Sermons
for
Special
Occasions

Publishing House
St. Louis

Concordia Publishing House, St. Louis, Missouri
Copyright © 1981 Concordia Publishing House

Manufactured in the United States of America

2 3 4 5 6 7 8 9 10 WP 90 89 88 87 86 85 84 83 82

Library of Congress Cataloging in Publication Data

Sermons for special occasions.

Includes bibliographical references.
1. Occasional sermons. 2. Sermons, American.
3. Lutheran Church—Sermons. I. Concordia Publishing House, St. Louis.
BV4254.2.S43   252'.6   80-25118
ISBN 0-570-03825-1

PREFACE

Many special occasions in the life of the church—19 of which are noted in this book—are not covered by homiletical aids dealing with the church year lectionary. When the need arises for a sermon in such a case, the insights of other preachers can be helpful. This collection of sermons is herewith offered as an available friend in such a need.

An additional feature of this volume is the listing of parallel texts and/or Scripture readings and suggested hymns to fit the sermon.

May these sermons provide a fitting Gospel word to special occasions that occur in the lives of God's people.

The Publisher

CONTRIBUTORS

Gerhard Aho
Fort Wayne, IN

Lloyd L. Behnken
Longwood, FL

Ronald W. Brusius
St. Louis, MO

Victor A. Constien
St. Louis, MO

Kenneth L. Frerking
Columbia, MO

Ernest L. Gerike
Bloomington, IL

James T. Hoppes
Fort Dodge, IA

Kent R. Hunter
Detroit, MI

W. Theophil Janzow
Seward, NE

Richard G. Kapfer
Ames, IA

Erwin J. Kolb
Troy, IL

Bruce J. Lieske
Fond du Lac, WI

Willard A. Roth
St. Louis, MO

Martin H. Scharlemann
St. Louis, MO

Theodore W. Schroeder
St. Louis, MO

Paul Ph. Spitz
St. Louis, MO

Michael J. Stelmachowicz
Seward, NE

Leland R. Stevens
St. Louis, MO

Jaroslav J. Vajda
St. Louis, MO

CONTENTS

THEMES, OCCASIONS, TEXTS, AND AUTHORS

75th CHURCH ANNIVERSARY

A Diamond for His Crown

REV. 19:5-9, 11-16

Happy anniversary! Happy wedding anniversary! Today we are celebrating the 75th anniversary of a marriage! What a long time since the wedding, and how long since the courtship and honeymoon! Today you are the bride, and together we will try to recall how this marriage came about. The Groom is having no trouble at all remembering. His eyes light up as He reviews the first time He met you; He can never forget how His bride looked on their wedding day, all lovely and radiant.

That was a long time ago. Suppose it was your own wedding you were remembering today. What would you recall? How you looked as a bride—how you met your husband—your dreams of the future—the joys and hardships of your marriage? Your children and their children?

Some marriages have only years to count: long stretches of dullness and boredom and silent separation that never becomes public because of dread as to what the public will say. But inwardly, they have been hatching an empty egg. It'd been a lot of work and busyness, but they have little to show for all the years they spent together: no sense of achievement, no grand and glorious memories.

But you, [name of congregation], as bride today recall your marriage to your Lord and Savior. If you could travel back in a time capsule to the year 1905 and witness the wedding in the era of horse-drawn carriages and trolleys, hoop skirts and crinoline, bowlers and narrow trousers—what a rustle and commotion, what excitement and dreams when this marriage was planned and the wedding day finally arrived. there she was, the bride—full of anticipation and fresh hopes, all ready to walk down the aisle to meet her Groom.

And the Groom! Let's not forget His part in this marriage. A groom often occupies second place in the limelight of the wedding, but not this One. He was the One who found her. The bride was in love with Him and He with her. He had courted her and won her and now they were to be one! What a couple they made! If you could see what would happen in the years to come, you would have noticed the Groom far outclassed the bride. He was way too good for her. He was the greatest catch any girl could hope to get—and He was yours!

In fact, that was one of the few royal weddings [place] was privileged to entertain, for it was a King who had come to this town to pick His bride. His eyes flamed like fire and on His head He wore a sparkling, dazzling crown, heavy with gold and precious stones. And the clothes He wore were drenched in blood! Can you imagine such a Bridegroom? If the bride was aware of this at all, she was awed to think that this great Hero, this King returning from victorious battle for her, was to be her Husband. What an honor, what an awesome elevation, what a special occasion!

Think of it—this Savior by whom all are redeemed, this King, who is Lord over all the creatures and rulers of this world—this is your Husband to have and to hold, to love and cherish, not till death do you part, but for anniversaries without end!

There are times in most marriages when a wife must wonder if she made the right choice. She sees other marriages that seem to be so much happier and rewarding. So the Christian church also has occasional doubts as to whether being joined to her husband Jesus Christ is really the best match. So many other associations seem to be more successful and popular and less demanding than the fellowship of the Christian church. And sometimes the bride shows her doubts about her marriage by her lukewarmness toward her Husband, by small ways of ignoring Him, by not centering her life and interests around Him, but rather practicing a kind of open marriage that is really nothing more than a casual relationship in which the communication becomes one-sided and there is only a random word or look toward the Spouse, and the "I love yous" dwindle until they become "I love" and then only "I." The struggle in this marriage is against overwhelming odds and mountainous disappointments. But this is the time to take another look at your Husband—Groom in the perspective of the picture in our text.

He is no self-centered man whose only aim in life is to come home to his castle house and sit in front of the TV, or merely satisfy his selfish interests. This Husband of yours had a destiny. That's why His wedding garment is drenched in blood. He has come through a life and death struggle with all the forces that would have separated you from Him forever. While you were waiting to be found and your thoughts were miles away from anyone like Him, He was busy tearing away the obstacles that stood between you and Him. He even died in that struggle—but, special and wondrous Champion that He is, He throttled death and got up from the very grave alive. That was the destiny He had. But He continues to have a destiny beyond that victory. He has been crowned the omnipotent King and Lord of all. And this is not an empty or cardboard title, the kind we shrink in value when we bestow it on ordinary and weak mortals in our clubs and societies. This Lord of lords has the authority and government of all the nations whom He rules in perfect justice and judgment. That's why He wears that crown. He is worthy to judge all because He has redeemed all. Everything and everyone is His. Those who delight in this claim of His, love and serve Him. And He will even the score for His own in the end, making up for all their sacrifices and proving they were right in being loyal to Him.

This is the Groom this congregation became married to 75 years ago. This is the Husband who loves you more than a man loves his brother. C. S. Lewis said that when people complain that God does not love them enough, they are really complaining that He loves them too much. The kind of love your heavenly Bridegroom has for you will not leave you alone or desert you. If you wanted a perfect Husband who loves with a perfect love, that's what you got. Anyone who is bound by ths kind of love is under lifelong obligation to Him. And this obligation of love can be either willing and cheerful or reluctant and stifling. This may help to explain some of the ups and downs in the history of this congregation. When the service was cheerful and appreciative, realizing who the Husband is, the impact on the community and the rewards in your own life were beyond measuring. When the love cooled off—because you momentarily forgot to whom you were married—the service to Him was halfhearted and the impact you made on others with your love was weak at best.

Much of happy marriage consists in remembering. You can be sure your Groom keeps on remembering what you are to Him. You are doing something today that should be a regular habit, too.

Today we are remembering two kinds of marriage: the marriage of this congregation to Christ, and the marriage of the members of this church then and now. We wouldn't be celebrating this event today if our grandparents had not married and had families and gathered other families to join them, and then carried out the purpose of marriage: they had children and raised families and their children's families in turn kept the congregation going and growing.

Keeping a marriage going is no easy matter, any more than keeping a congregation going. You need a lot of inspiration and patience, you need a goal, and you need daily forgiveness. There are many times in the life of a family when you wonder if it's worth all the bother and sacrifice, whether it matters if your marriage succeeds or whether your family counts. Who notices what you are doing, your children don't all become famous, others have enough problems of their own and don't care what happens to you?

But marriages and families do matter. We were created to belong to a family, and marriage is a normal desire for most people. In fact, a country or society would quickly disintegrate if people stopped getting married and forming families. There has to be a place where an infant can get a good start and grow in a supportive atmosphere. There has to be a place where values are learned, and where love is experienced from people who care about others.

The model for our marriages and families is the church. "Husbands, love your wives, even as Christ also loved the church, and gave Himself for it." "Wives, submit yourselves unto your own husbands, as unto the Lord." Bring up your children "in the nurture and admonition of the Lord." (Eph. 5:25, 22; 6:4 KJV). In the marriage of Christ to the church we have a model for successful marriages and rewarding and beneficial families.

If you were meant not to marry—or to marry and not have children— you were still meant to be married to Christ and to know the relationship of God's family—and you can bear children for God in that marriage as St. Paul did though he was a bachelor, yet he counted many Christians as his children in Christ.

As members of the Christian family, we are providing the world with a model for society's survival and happiness. We are creating a shelter and nest where the lonely orphans of the world can find a homey atmosphere of acceptance and love and friendship as so many have in this congregation.

I tell you frankly this is what I am looking for when I go to this church or any other: I'm looking for the love of Christ demonstrated in His church and the commitment of the church to her Savior. I'm looking for a model marriage between Christ and His church, and the family values that result from it. This is what happens when college students, service people, and Christians who move to another location find in a new church home—a family away from home. And often a person will find in the church family better ideals than he finds at home and more acceptance than he finds in his own family.

So, as a congregation marking its diamond anniversary, we have a lot to celebrate today. Not all 75 years were lived on the same level of intensity as the first ones. There were many warm moments in those 75 years and also many sorrowful and regrettable ones, separations and disappointments, and some children leaving the family never to return.

You have a few things to repent, you have some vows to repeat, and some love and zeal to recapture. You must remember that for this Husband-King you are a diamond in His crown. When people see you, they see the degree of love and devotion you have toward your Groom. You are chosen to glorify Him and to rule with Him.

We have all noticed how so many long-married couples get to look like each other more and more. At least, if they are very much in love and enjoy a close relationship, they almost think alike. They can practically read each others minds, and often they will do the wishes of the other without being asked. Every marriage should have this kind of intimacy and communication. For a Christian congregation, this kind of closeness between the church and her Groom can be a growing and lasting experience. And when you sense it now and then, it's enough to make you cry for joy that such a rare and heavenly thing can happen to you.

In one sense I have been stretching the comparison of the marriage of the church to Christ in including the congregation. But you and we are the bride of Christ even as a local congregation insofar as we are His chosen redeemed who have been baptized into His name. And what can be said of one congregation, can be said of many. Remember King Solomon with his thousand wives. Each of them could claim him as her husband-king. He wrote a long song in which he exchanged intimate sentiments with his beloved Shumanite. What a love affair that was. But Jesus said: "One greater than Solomon is here," meaning Himself.

This Solomon is the Husband of many thousands of brides. And each wife is like a diamond in His crown. And the relationship to each is as close as that of a lover with his beloved. The Song of Solomon is the song of Jesus, the Lover of your soul, and you, His beloved bride.

I have also connected this anniversary to Revelation 19, which speaks of the wedding of the Lamb on the day of judgment. There is a real unity between each Christian and Christ, and between each local congregation and Christ, and each marriage and Christ as a preview or foretaste of that great marriage. (vv. 4-10) Just as each communion celebration is a foretaste of the Supper we will eat and drink with the Lamb in heaven.

So then, enjoy and celebrate this marriage, which now marks its diamond anniversary. Recall your first love and renew it. Your Husband-Lover-King and Lord is as loving as ever. In 75 years you have hardly begun to exhaust the joy of being His bride.

Diamonds are precious. They are not plastic or Zircon imitations that are cheaply bought. One soul is more precious to Jesus than all the minerals in this world. For one He would give everything He has—and that's exactly what He did for you who are His diamonds.

Diamonds are forever. They retain their value when all other artifacts of man are crumbled in ruins and decayed. He has made you His diamonds and sustained you until your diamond anniversary.

You are a diamond for His Crown! You have been placed into it by a glorious plan. You have been worked into it lovingly and with great care. And you are in that crown forever.

Sparkle and gleam, glitter and glorify Him as a diamond in His crown. Amen.   Jaroslav J. Vajda

Related Scripture reading
Eph. 5:21-33

Suggested hymns
"Now Thank We All Our God"
"Oh, Blest the House, Whate'er Befall"
"For All the Saints"
"Crown Him with Many Crowns"

BACCALAUREATE/GRADUATION

A Proper Goal for a Christian Graduate

MARK 10:43-45

Graduation is a signal event in the life of any educational institution. It means the fulfillment of its basic purpose. Schools exist to help students learn. They want to impart knowledge. They want to teach skills. They want to shape attitudes. To announce that a class is ready to graduate means that the faculty of the school has determined that the members of the class have reached the levels of learning represented by the diplomas they will receive. This is a happy event for any faculty. It means that the purpose of the institution is being accomplished.

Graduation, however, has special meaning also for the student, the graduate. In fact, it is rich in meaning on the individual level because it can have many meanings for the same person, but it may also mean different things to different people.

Each graduate has finished a course of studies required for his or her diploma. But each had a somewhat different experience. For some it was easy; for others hard. Some used the experience to learn just as much as they could; others were satisfied with "just getting by." Some had their goals spelled out all the way and even now know exactly where they are headed, perhaps not realizing that sometimes the Lord has new and unexpected directions for us to go. Others did not find quick and easy answers to what they wanted to do after graduation and perhaps even now, on this occasion, may still be waiting for the clear voice of direction regarding their life's work. A graduating class is like a patchwork quilt, which the dictionary defines as a needlework cover made out of odd pieces of cloth, sewn together at the edges. So each person in this class has had his or her separate experiences, comes to this graduation having developed into a unique and distinctive personality, and yet is tied to their classmates by the bond of common class affiliation.

But from here on out it's a new life and a new world. The most important question of this moment isn't "What about the past?" but "Where to from here"? What direction will you take now? What are your goals?

It would be impossible for me to use this sermon to advise you on an individual level. But I can set before you a general principle. And this I hope now to do, basing my remarks on Mark 10:43-45, and organizing my thoughts around the theme: "A Proper Goal for Christian Graduates."

I

My first emphasis, in elaborating on this topic, is basically negative. It says quite bluntly: "Don't let power and riches become the chief reason for your existence on this earth."

In making this suggestion I know that I am going against the secular stream of our times. One author, in a popular book of a couple of decades ago, (Vance Packard, *Status Seekers)* says that we are a nation of status seekers. People want to "get up in the world." A frequent objective of new graduates is to "get to the top" just as fast as possible. Why is status considered so desirable? One of the reasons is that it gives people power.

Furthermore, it has long been known that America's economic system, which has provided a high level of affluence to the majority of our citizens, at the same time often shapes people's value judgments in such a way that their main goal in life is making money. A major Midwest newspaper *(Omaha World—Herald)* took a poll at the first of the year (published Jan. 1, 1980) and found that 68 percent of the population gives moneymaking a high rating in the things they consider important in this life.

This means that two goals drive many people in their occupational and professional careers: money and power.

Our text helps us to analyze how these widespread goals in our culture fit into the kind of value system that can be called Christian.

James and John wanted to be disciples of Christ. They, in fact, were disciples of Christ. They certainly would have wanted other people to think of them as Christians.

On one occasion, they too, just like this graduating class, were looking ahead, were trying to crystallize their goals, and were trying to state in summary fashion what, in the final analysis, they hoped to achieve in their lives.

Sometimes people couch their baser desires and their coarser ambitions in euphemisms, in nice-sounding phrases that try to attach a soft, pleasing melody to the harsh music rumbling around in their souls.

Not so James and John. They came right out with it. Whether from naivete, ignorance, or sheer greed we do not know. But they threw it right into the group in its crassest form, without trying to meet or muffle their selfish ambitions. They said simply, "We want to be with You at the top. Our goal is to be Your chief lieutenants, one on Your right hand, the other on Your left, when You ascend to Your throne in glory." (Mark 10:37). It was clear that they had shown their hand. Their goal was power and certainly all that goes with it.

We're not going to get into the question of whether they were thinking of a political kingdom or a spiritual one. Quite possibly their ambitions included both.

The greater question is: Were they on the right track? Were they justified? Were their ambitions consonant with how Christians should order their lives and line up their goals?

Jesus gives a clear and unequivocal answer. He says: "it shall not be so among you; but whoever would be great among you must be your servant, and whoever would be first among you must be slave of all" (Mark 10:43-44 RSV).

James and John, we must point out, were not unique in succumbing to the power and glory syndrome as the organizing principle of their lives. We find it on a worldwide basis. We find it in every age. We find it both outside and inside the church. We find it rampant in our civilization today.

Basically, it's the drive that is imbedded in the deepest core of our sinful nature. You may call it pride. You may call it greed. You may call it selfishness. The specific name is not important. That one recognizes it when it rises in one's heart, that's what counts.

And when one recognizes it, what does one do with it? From time immemorial people have tried to convince themselves and others that it's OK, it's moral, it's Christian, to make power, riches, and glory their main goal in life.

But saying so doesn't make it true. Examples of lives that have demonstrated that blind ambition is basically destructive are almost endless. The worst examples, Genghis Khan, Hitler, and, of more recent vintage, Jim Jones only tend to lend some credence to the dictum of a 19th-century philosopher (Lord Acton): "Power tends to corrupt, and absolute power corrupts absolutely."

But, if power and riches and glory are not proper primary objectives for a Christian's life, what is?

II

This brings us to the other, the positive, emphasis of this sermon. What is a proper goal for a Christian graduate? I can give you a one word answer. It is "service."

Let us hear again what Jesus said. "Whoever would be great among you must be your servant, and whoever would be first among you must be slave of all" (Mark 10:43-44 RSV).

Jesus didn't only make this statement as a theoretical proposition. He presented His own life as a living illustration.

Jesus reminded His disciples that "the Son of man also came not to be served but to serve" (Mark 10:45 RSV). And they knew it was true. They had witnessed His life dedicated to the service of His fellow man. They had seen Him help the poor, feed the hungry, comfort the sick and sorrowing, treat outcasts with kindness, ignite a spark of hope in the hearts of those who felt downtrodden and rejected. They had seen Him spend hours upon hours giving personal attention to people who came in droves with their troubles and their griefs. Just by watching Him they should have known. And when Jesus pointed this out to them they must have said to themselves: "What fools we have been, to think that power and glory is where it's at. All we had to do is look at Jesus and we could have known. Anyone who wants to follow in His footsteps must put service at the head of his ambitions list."

People in this audience, I suppose, are going to wonder whether or how it's possible to apply this in every Christian's life. How can everyone, regardless of calling or occupation, say: "I dedicate my life to service."

After all, not all Christians are going to choose one of the professions that are generally identified as the helping or service professions. Not all Christians are going to be nurses, social workers, or teachers, or in some other work that most people recognize as helping occupations. Some Christians will be business men, or corporate executives, or politicians, or financiers, or enter some other occupation in which power or money is usually perceived of as the primary goal.

To resolve this apparent dilemma, Christians must learn to understand that it's usually not the job that determines the primary driving forces in a human beings life. It's the motivation; it's the spirit; it's the heart.

A man in a position of power has a choice. He can use his influence to manipulate his fellowmen for his own benefit. Or he can use it to throw his weight around in the interest of service. That is, he can exert his influence so that the resources over which he has control can be used to the greatest extent possible, not to exploit human beings, but to help and serve them.

The same, of course, can be said for the wealthy man. The point is, it doesn't make any difference. Are you going to be doctor, lawyer, merchant, or chief? Are you going to be butcher, baker, or candlestick maker? If you want to be whatever you are in a Christlike way, then you will say: "I'm going to make service the primary goal in my life's career or work."

Nobody, of course, can carry it as far as Jesus did. He carried it to the cross. He took our sins so that we could get rid of them. He suffered hell so that we could enjoy heaven. He died so that we could live. Nobody else could do that. He could, as the Son of God. He could, as the Savior of the world. He could, as the one who, having died, wou'd rise again and share His everlasting life with us so that we would never have to die. Jesus, therefore, served as the perfect model of the perfect Servant.

We can never match His marvelous ministry. But believing in Him, drawing limited energy from His inexhaustible power, we can try to follow after. We can imitate. We can, as Luther said, be little servants, little Christs.

A life dedicated to the principle of service seldom pays as well, seldom brings in as much profit as a life dedicated to making money. But it is rich in personal satisfaction; it is powerful in helping people understand how Christian love works; and it is the true way for us as Christians to organize our lives because that is the way Christ our Lord and Savior organized His.

Graduates sometimes like to think in terms of mottos. One of the best mottos, or statements of purpose, that I can leave with you as you think about your future after graduation is found in the fourth verse of the famous hymn by Genevieve Irons. Having witnessed to her faith in Jesus Christ as her crucified Redeemer she concludes:

> And then for work to do for Thee,
> Which shall so sweet a service be
> That angels well might envy me,
>   Christ Crucified, I come. *(The Lutheran Hymnal* 390:4)

May that also be the goal that you set or renew on your graduation day. Amen.   W. Theophil Janzow

Related Scripture readings

Deut. 10:12-15	Phil. 2:1-11	John 13:12-17
Ps. 2	Gal. 6:7-10	Matt. 5:13-16
Ps. 100	1 Peter 2:11-21	Luke 10:25-37

Suggested hymns

"Our God, Our Help in Ages Past"
"Drawn to the Cross"
"Take My Life and Let It Be"
"May We Thy Precepts, Lord, Fulfill"
"Oh, that the Lord Would Guide My Ways"

CHRISTIAN EDUCATION

Our Mandate to Educate

COL. 2:6-7

Our beliefs and lifestyle as individuals and as members of this parish are being tested. It's not unusual for Christians to face such challenges, of course. But the fact is that antagonism toward Christian ethical standards is becoming more open, and skepticism of Christian teachings and practices is growing. Many people criticize Christian goals for marriage and family life. Faithful participation in worship services and the Lord's Supper is ridiculed as obsolete tradition. Some people are overtly attacking Christian doctrines, such as the inherent sinfulness of human beings and the unending grace of God who freely justifies sinners, declaring them forgiven through faith in Jesus Christ alone. Others boldly reject the Holy Scriptures, refusing to accept them as the source and norm for Christian faith and life. Our own frailties have contributed to the fact that many are resisting the call of God to a religion that is pure and undefiled. We have confessed the creeds, but we have been slow to visit the orphans and widows in their affliction and to keep ourselves unspotted from the world.

Nevertheless, while these problems plague us, several promises of God encourage us. God has called us into a priesthood of believers. Brothers and sisters in Christ surround and support us. Through His reliable and altogether trustworthy Word, God the Holy Spirit continues to teach us. He enables us to know the truth about God and ourselves and our relationship to Him and one another. God has blessed us with insight into effective methods of teaching and learning His Gospel. He has also given us the opportunity and skill to develop various Christian education media for people of all age levels. Under His guidance the church has become aware of the need to evaluate its ministry of the Word of God to itself and the world and to overcome weaknesses and build on strengths, with a new sense of accountability to Him.

For the next few minutes we spend together here let's bring these problems and promises together. We can bolster one another with

Our Mandate to Educate

The Word of God that instructs us is from the second chapter of

Paul's Letter to the Colossians, especially verses 6 and 7: "As therefore you received Christ Jesus the Lord, so live in Him, rooted and built up in Him and established in the faith, just as you were taught, abounding in thanksgiving" (RSV).

The educational challenge we confront today is in at least one way similar to that which Paul confronted when he wrote to the Christians at Colossae. The people of that city wanted knowledge, wisdom, and understanding. They had curiosities to be satisfied and personal and social problems to be resolved. So they turned to those who promised enlightenment and help.

Among those who tendered their assistance were mystery cultists. They offered the privileges of intimate knowledge by which they promised personal salvation. Through the rites and ceremonies of their cults they invited people to taste the deliverance that—they said—only they could provide by walks along their private pathways of truth. They invited Christians, too. Of course, Jesus Christ also had a place within their systems, they said. They did not reject Him. But they claimed that they could lead people beyond Him. In addition to Jesus are many other angelic powers that can help people battle evil and do good, they said. Yes, Jesus had overcome sin for them, they agreed. But war still needed to be waged against cosmic evil agents. That called for self-sacrificing discipline, help from the angelic forces, and initiation into their cult with its exceptional knowledge.

What was Paul's answer to their false claims? "You have received Christ Jesus, the Lord," Paul wrote. Jesus is the source of wisdom and knowledge. He is not a mere first among equals. The fullness of God dwells in Jesus bodily. In Him people have the fullness of life. He is far above all the angels. He is the image of the invisible God.

Paul wanted the Colossians to remember what Jesus did, too. Through Him all things were created, in heaven and on earth, visible and invisible. He is the Creator of the angels, not simply one of their peers or partners. When Jesus set out to complete the Father's plan of salvation, He did not leave the job half done. He finished it. By His death in His body of flesh He reconciled and presented to God holy and blameless and irreproachable those who were estranged and hostile in mind, doing evil deeds. Paul reminded the Colossians that, as they continue in the faith, stable and steadfast, not shifting from the hope of the Gospel, they are saved. Nothing remains for people to do or for angels to do. Jesus has met and canceled the demand of God's law, nailing it to His cross. He has already conquered all evil powers. People need not try to defeat those forces as if it were their assignment. In His cross Jesus has already triumphed.

We contemporary Christians fail to carry out our mandate to educate when we teach and live as if salvation were through some special human effort or self-discipline or through mediation by anyone except Jesus. Then we are guilty of the Colossian heresy.

Our mandate to educate originates with what we have been taught: Jesus Christ is Savior and Lord. What He did by His life, death, and resurrection, He did for us. By our Baptism He joined us to Himself so that through faith in Him we have become His body. We have died with Him in His death to sin and death and all their power. In Him our lives are complete. In Him we are fulfilled. We need no additional, superior teaching to bring us to perfection. In Christ God has reconciled all things to Himself, making peace by the blood of His cross.

Our mandate to educate is lifelong. Paul's picture of the process is that of constructing a building. First, the foundation is planted deep and solid. Then out of the foundation the superstructure rises, built up of the stones, mortar, and wood that give it shape and hold it together. However, in Paul's picture the building process never stops. It continues throughout a person's life.

The foundation of life is already laid, once and for all, in Jesus. God intends no other. No other foundation can be laid than that which is laid in Him. In Jesus life is rooted. He is the solid Rock. The verb form Paul chose indicates that Jesus has been established as our Foundation. That part of the building is completed. But now the entire life that rises from that foundation through continuing activity is built up and becomes more firm by faith in Him. We're interpreting Paul's words faithfully when we feel the imperative: "You have received Christ Jesus from a faithful teacher. So live in Christ. By faith sink your life deeply into Him, your Foundation. Then keep on building your life. Keep growing more and more until you become firm in Him."

Our mandate to educate calls us to translate Christian convictions into action. In order to counteract the false teaching that permeates our culture, detracting from Christ and His salvation, we are called to grasp tightly the faith we were taught. But there's more to it than hanging on. Our knowledge of the faith that has been entrusted to us is to mulitiply. If there is an explosion of technical knowledge throughout the world today—and there is—our unique calling is to promote and experience for ourselves and among others an explosion of the knowledge of God and His grace to us in Christ. Paul carefully selected His words. He wanted his readers to get the message. Being established in the faith means moving from faith to greater faith to excelling in the faith. Paul's concern was that Christians more and more develop both their understanding of the meaning of God's Word to them and the skill to make faithful and creative application of that Word in their daily personal lives.

Some of us as children thought we had achieved excellence in the faith when we won games of Bible baseball in Sunday school. Some of us even felt that we had reached the point where we knew more about the

Bible than our classmates and therefore were superior to them. By the time we were in the sixth grade we had heard some Bible stories over and over again and were certain that we could learn nothing more from them. So we deceived ourselves into thinking that we could skip Sunday or weekday school or confirmation classes. Now where are we as adults? We have not yet altogether put away these childish things. We still frequently judge ourselves to be of such excellence that we need no longer acknowledge nor try to close the gap between where we are and where God has called us to be. And the gap widens.

Paul's solution for such misguided pride and self-honor may surprise us. While he urged the Colossians on to spiritual excellence, he knew how easily we are all tempted to think of ourselves more highly than we ought to think. So he wrote to the Colossians, "Live in Christ, rooted and built up in Him and established in the faith, just as you were taught, *abounding in thanksgiving.*" That's Paul! He evokes thanksgiving to God. He focuses our attention where it belongs, not on ourselves and whatever excellence in the faith we may achieve, but on God, the giver of every good and perfect gift, including the gift of our faith. Thanksgiving to God begins when we penitently confess: "Nothing in my hand I bring . . . Naked come to Thee for dress. Helpless look to Thee for grace." Thanksgiving grows when we look away from ourselves to Him who provides mercy through the death and resurrection of Christ Jesus. From Him alone comes the power to grow in grace and in the knowledge of our Lord Jesus Christ. Therefore, if there is any commendation, any praise or honor for excellence in faith, it belongs to Him.

Our mandate to educate, abounding in thanksgiving, involves every member of our parish as both a learner and a teacher. Whatever our ages, by sharing our experiences in the grace of God we can teach one another of that grace. Because we have all had different experiences we can, under the Holy Spirit's directive, learn from one another. That's why one of the best ways to describe our congregation is to call it a "teaching-learning community."

Sometimes we have reduced our potential for learning by treating Christian education as if it were only something for the children. And often then we have cheated the children by merely holding classes where teachers do all the talking and the children just sit and listen. We have promoted Bible class for our young people in order to "Keep them with the church." That's good, but it's not enough. Our ministry with young people is to enable them to sustain one another and us all with their knowledge of God and their skills of service. In our adult Bible classes we may have spent too much time trying to help men and women review and recall what they have forgotten since confirmation when we should have been spending more time equipping them to share what they remember for building up the whole company of believers.

The congregations of The Lutheran Church—Missouri Synod, meeting in convention, have underscored the need to involve all their members in teaching and learning the good news of Christ. Here's how they put it: "Christian education is a lifelong process. Spiritual growth is both necessary and possible at all age levels. A formal program of Christian education provides positive influence for Christian teaching and learning. We affirm that in the process of Christian education every member of the church must be both teacher and learner."

Our mandate to educate will be fulfilled in our congregation to the extent that we show loving respect for each learner and faithfully select, train, and sustain effective teachers. From time to time, especially when I am with volunteer teachers of Sunday, weekday, or confirmation classes, I ask, "Do you remember any Christian teacher from your childhood? If so, what do you remember most about that particular teacher?" Think about that a minute for yourself. Now tell that person sitting next to you why you remember that person especially. Or maybe you have a favorite Sunday school teacher in one of the classes you attend now. Why do you like that teacher?—I couldn't hear all your conversations, of course, so I can't tabulate all the responses to the question. But your answers are probably similar to those I have heard on other occasions. We like and remember teachers who treat us like we are somebody important. They take time to listen to us and personally to show us love. They know the Bible and are still growing in it. They know that they are loved by Jesus and they love Jesus. They show it by caring about us. Those are the kind of teachers God is raising up by the power of His Spirit in our congregation, our teaching-learning community. We praise God for you. Within our fellowship no single group of people has more influence than you, our teachers.

To enable all of us to confront antagonism, skepticism, unbelief, false teaching, and immorality we have received a mandate from God. That mandate is to educate. From our own faithful teachers, like the Colossians' Epaphras and Paul, we have received Christ Jesus the Lord. Now by faith, with our lives sunk deeply into Him, our Foundation, we are called to keep building our lives in Him, growing more and more until we become firm in Him. Amen.   Victor A. Constien

Related Scripture readings

Deut. 6:4-7	Matt. 28:16-20	Rom. 12:1-13
Ps. 119:9-16	John 21:15-19	Eph. 4:1-16

Suggested hymns

"Speak Forth Thy Word, O Father"
"Soldiers of the Cross, Arise"
"Gracious Savior, Gentle Shepherd"
"Let Children Hear the Mighty Deeds"

CONFIRMATION

Confirmation Days: Days of Stretching

JOHN 14:23-29

I suppose that if you have been confirmed in the Lutheran church, a morning like this brings back many memories. If you want to see how you have changed and grown, just look at your confirmation picture! You children will do the same thing some day, looking at your confirmation picture and laughing at the way you looked today. Although you look very nice, you are going to do some more growing, and you are going to be putting on some weight, and later on getting some lines in your faces. Things will change very much over the years.

Confirmation day is an important day, because it is on that day that young people make a public affirmation of their faith in the Triune God, Father, Son, and Holy Spirit. They are saying that they will continue to follow after Jesus, but on a new plateau. It is not as though these children are saying that now they are becoming Christians, for they have been Christians ever since the day they were received into God's kingdom by Holy Baptism. Their faith in Jesus Christ is what makes them members of the holy Christian Church. Now they are on a new plateau of their discipleship.

Our text for this morning describes another "confirmation class," if you will. This class consists of the disciples of Jesus, meeting around a Passover meal on Maundy Thursday. Jesus had gathered His disciples because He wanted to prepare them for some big events that were about to happen—the events of that evening and especially of Good Friday, the next day. John records the words of Jesus in this way: "I have told you this now before it all happens, so that when it does happen, you will ·believe" (John 14:29 TEV).

Jesus knew that His disciples were going to be facing some "stretched-out times" in which they would feel like a rubber band stretched almost to the point of breaking.

If confirmation means to affirm on a new level and with new insights our faith in Jesus Christ, if it means that we have reached a point where we have grown and realized that we have grown, if it means that it is a time when we affirm in a stronger way our being followers of Jesus

Christ, then confirmation should not be spoken of in the *singular* but in the *plural*. It is a plural word because there are all kinds of stretching, growing, and new plateau days in our lives. We are stretched out in those days, and God's grace is stretched out even further to cover us. When those stretching days are over we can look back and realize that we have truly grown because of the experience. *That* is a confirmation day. These confirmation days happen more and more to Christians in the age in which we live today. So we celebrate the confirmation day of this confirmation class, and we also celebrate our own confirmation days under the theme:

Confirmation Days: Days of Stretching
I. Stretching Toward Obedience

When you children were growing up, your parents may have propped you up against a wall where a growth chart had been taped and measured your height on your birthday. They would take a ruler and mark your growth, and then you would turn around and look at how much you had grown since your last birthday. Pretty soon your parents will no longer mark your growth, because you will have attained your adult height. Yet it is fun to mark off growth.

When we enter the stretching times that I referred to before, it is often difficult to realize that those kinds of days are happening. It is much more difficult to measure. However, there are marks of stretching that we can see. The disciples could observe one of these marks on that Maundy Thursday. They felt pain. They felt fright. They felt anticipation. Jesus had told them that He was going to leave them and then return to them. They did not know what this meant. But they did know that this was a time when they would be entering the unknown. That is the first mark of a stretched-out time. It is time when we are entering the unknown, a time and place we haven't been before.

We know that you confirmands will enter many stretching times in your teens and your young adult years. Because of this we are praying for you. We are wondering whether or not you will be faithful to your Lord Jesus in those times. Will you follow after your Master? Will you apply the Gospel to real life situations? We know that the devil, the world, and your own sinful flesh will oppose the new life that you have in Jesus Christ. You are entering stretched-out days in which you will face the unknown.

For all of us there are those same kinds of stretched-out days. There is the question mark that a student faces who comes to the university for the first time and confronts the unknown. Question marks confront a young man and woman as they prepare for marriage, wondering if they will be a good husband and wife. Questions arise when one's first child is born, when one wonders if one will be the God-pleasing parent one wants to be. Questions arise when we are left alone because of a death in our family or because the "nest" is emptied and our children grow up and away from us. Questions arise when trials and temptations come to us and we wonder whether we can face them. Questions arise when we begin to accumulate enough wealth so that we can purchase possessions, and we wonder if we will become materialistic. All of these days are filled with questions. These are the days of the unknown.

The second sign that a stretched-out time is coming is when we realize that the familiar is no longer there. The disciples certainly must have experienced that on Maundy Thursday. Whereas Jesus had been so popular, with many people following Him and adding to the joyful enthusiasm that the disciples had, now many people were falling away from Him because they began to realize the meaning of following after Jesus. The disciples had thought that the kingdom that Jesus would bring would be a kingdom of this world. Now Jesus was telling them that He would leave them. How can you build an earthly kingdom when you are not there to reign over it? The disciples were entering the unfamiliar. Everything was changing.

You confirmands are entering that kind of unfamiliar territory— reaching out for young adulthood. How all of us—parents, members of this congregation, grandparents, and sponsors—would like to smooth the way for you! We cannot do that. For His disciples Jesus prayed: "I do not pray that Thou shouldst take them out of the world, but that Thou shouldst keep them from the evil one" (John 17:15 RSV). That is our prayer for you as you enter unfamiliar times. We are praying that you will remain faithful to your faithful God.

The unfamiliar time is when we find that the kingdom of God is on a collision course with the kingdom of this world and find that we must ask some basic questions about our lives. We cannot stand where we stood before. The whole territory has been changed.

When that time comes, Jesus says to us, as He said to His disciples: "I require one thing of you, and that is that you *obey.*" This is what Jesus is saying in our text, "Whoever loves Me will obey My teaching" (v. 23 TEV). Yet Jesus does not give a particular rule to obey. He does not say, "Here's the law that you must follow when the stretched-out time comes." He does not say this because there are no rules for the unknown and unfamiliar except this word of Jesus: "Follow Me!" That's what we take into the stretched-out times: "Follow Me!"

Look at the words that Jesus uses when He talks about this obedience. "My Father will love him, and My Father and I will come to live with him" (v. 23 TEV). Such personal terms from our personal God! In the midst of the stretched-out times, He says to us, "Follow Me! Because I live in you, I call on you to follow Me." That's what fills the void, the emptiness, the unknown. Our Lord gives us a place to stand. The best place to stand in a stretched-out time is to stand in the footprints of Jesus, ready to follow Him. That's the most powerful advice that one can give for any days of stretching.

II. Stretching Toward Remembrance

When we follow Jesus, He gives us a specific and certain promise. This promise is guaranteed. It will happen also to you. Jesus said to His disciples, "I have told you this while I am still with you. The Helper, the Holy Spirit, whom the Father will send in My name, will teach you *everything* and make you *remember* all that I have told you" (vv. 25-26, TEV). Jesus is saying that in the stretched-out times, "I will send you a Friend. His name is Paraclete." That is the literal translation for the word "helper." It means to "call to one's side." A Friend comes to us in the unknown and unfamiliar. He is by our side and lets us know that He is there. The name of this Paraclete is known to us better by the words, "Holy Spirit," the "Comforter."

Why can we be confident about the members of our confirmation class? Because they have the Holy Spirit living within them by faith in their Lord Jesus Christ. Why can people face some extremely stretched-out times in their lives and come out strengthened in their faith? It is because of the Holy Spirit. And how is it that we will, in fact, be able to face situations about which we would say beforehand, "I could never go through that!" It is because our Paraclete, the Holy Spirit, our Friend, is going to be with us. In the moment of our greatest need, our Friend comes to us.

Where do we find this Friend? God tells us that His gift of the Holy Spirit comes in small packages. He is found in the Holy Scriptures and in Holy Communion, where we receive the Lord's body and blood. That's where power is found for the powerless. That is where our Friend comes to our side to be with us in stretched-out places.

That, of course, is where our problem also lies. Because He comes in the small packages of Word and Sacrament, we tend not to trust the power of the Paraclete. Peter did not, and in the stretched-out place of that Maundy Thursday evening, he drew out his sword and tried to depend on that kind of power. Judas had gone away from the Upper Room that evening to betray his Lord, depending upon money in the stretched-out time of his life. All the disciples fled into the night on that stretched-out evening time. That will be our problem also in the stretched-out times. We will want to reach out and push the button of power. We will want to push on the button of the cash register. We will want to turn the key of our own hiding place. But then, by the grace of God, perhaps our Lord will bring us to our senses and the Holy Spirit will come to us in His small packages and bring to our remembrance all that our Lord has spoken to us. Then the Paraclete will remind us of what God has said to each one of us: "I have called you by name; you are Mine" (Is. 43:1 RSV).

III. Stretching Toward Peace

The days that followed Maundy Thursday were at first extremely ugly days. The disciples had never been so stretched out! They saw their Lord betrayed, tried, crucified, and buried. Then they experienced the explosion of Easter's joy. After this they saw their Lord ascend into heaven, and then the Holy Spirit did indeed come to them on Pentecost. It was at this point that they could look back to where they had been on Maundy Thursday. What tremendous growth had occurred! How they had been changed! How the stretched-out days had prepared them for this new vista, this new experience, this new day that was preparing them for even more growth!

Our Lord is always with us. He is there in the midst of the stretched-out days, understanding our needs and helping us all along the way. We may feel that we are stretched so tightly that we will break, but our Lord's grace is stretched even farther, drawing us farther than we ever dreamed we could go and stretching us into fuller and richer and better children of our heavenly Father than we had ever been before.

When this happens to us, we begin to understand what Jesus said to His disciples: "Peace is what I leave with you; it is My own peace that I give you. I do not give it as the world does. Do not be worried and upset; do not be afraid" (John 14:27 TEV).

This is the peace that we will also find when the stretched-out days have reached their fulfillment in a new confirmation day. We will be able to look back and know that our Lord was truly with us in every one of the stretched-out days. We will realize that the Paraclete did in fact come to our side in order to direct and guide us along every step of the way. We'll know that no matter how stretched out we have become, God has stretched even farther to assure us that "all things work together for good to those who love God." When that day comes, you will know that a confirmation day has occurred. You will know that you have grown. You will know that the Lord is truly directing your life. You will know that your life is totally in His hands. When that day comes, you will also be ready for new days of stretching, new days of growth, and new confirmation days.

There is one more promise that I can share with you, especially with the members of our confirmation class, because it is a promise that God has given to all of us. The promise is this: There is a final confirmation day that Peter, John, and all of the other disciples are already celebrating. That is the day on which we will be confirmed in heaven before our Lord, to be with Him, our life and our Light forever. Then the stretched-out days will be over, for we will be "stretched" into life everlasting. That's a promise to all who believe! What a confirmation day that will be! Amen.   Richard G. Kapfer

Related Scripture readings

Prov. 8:11-31	Luke 9:57-62	1 Cor. 15:58
Luke 2:41-52	John 15:1-10	Eph. 3:14-21
Luke 6:43-49	Rom. 6:5-11	

Suggested Hymns

"Blessed Savior, Who Hast Taught Me"
"My God, Accept My Heart This Day"
"Our Lord and God, Oh, Bless This Day"
"Thine Forever, God of Love"
"My God, My Father, Make Me Strong"
"Come, Follow Me, the Savior Spake"
"Let Us Ever Walk with Jesus"

CHURCH CORNERSTONE LAYING

Praise God for His Temples

EZRA 3:10-11

One of the most beautiful buildings in the world is the Taj Mahal, built in Agra, India, by the Muslim ruler Shah Jahan in the 17th century. It memorializes the Shah's wife, who died in 1631. Diamonds, sapphires, amethysts, and turquoises adorn the walls of this world-renowned structure. More than 20,000 men worked on it for many years. But it is only a mausoleum, dedicated to a memory and existing as a monument of praise to the master builders and architects who constructed it.

Today we praise God for two of His temples: the physical structure whose cornerstone we are about to lay and the spiritual temple that is the church—made up of people.

The Physical Temple

What a glorious moment it was when the builders of the second Jewish temple laid the foundation. The priests came forward blowing trumpets, Levites stepped forward with clashing cymbals, and there was much singing. The temple of Solomon had been destroyed by the

Babylonian armies in 586 B. C. The foundation was laid for the second temple in 520 B. C. and some scholars believe that the second temple was completed and dedicated in 516 B. C.—leaving a 70-year period during which God's people had no central location of worship. We, who desire so strongly our own new building, can well imagine how they felt when they laid the foundation stone for the new temple. It is important to note that they *praised the Lord* in their moment of "cornerstone laying." Their praise was enthusiastic. "All the people shouted with a great shout, when they praised the Lord, because the foundation of the house of the Lord was laid" (Ezra 3:11 KJV).

They praised *God* for their new house of worship—not the builders. We do not wish to take away any deserved praise from the architect and builders of our own building, but it is important to praise and thank God above all for this new building. He allowed us to come this far. By His Holy Spirit He stirred up people to assemble together as a congregation. He motivated people to be generous in financial support for this project. And we trust God to see this work to completion, believing the psalmist who wrote, "Unless the Lord builds the house, those who build it labor in vain" (Ps. 127:1 RSV).

We praise God for this new building today and recognize that it belongs to Him. We are only stewards of the property and building.

Because it is God's building, we will want to keep it clean and in good repair in the years to come. It is easy for us to treat our own property better than that of the church. Shortly before the foundation of the second Jewish temple was laid, the people of Israel had been apathetic about building the temple. They had returned to the land of Israel and were struggling financially. They had not the will to rebuild the temple. That was when the prophet Haggai said:

> It is a time for you yourselves to dwell in your paneled houses, while this house lies in ruins? Now therefore thus says the Lord of hosts: Consider how you have fared. You have sown much, and harvested little . . . and he who earns wages earns wages to put them into a bag with holes (Haggai 1:4-6 RSV).

Here is a warning to us not to despise or ignore the need to help pay the building costs of this church and the need for proper maintenance when it is finished.

We must, however, not overemphasize the building at the expense of more important Kingdom matters. The church building is a *means* to an end. The physical temple, or building, is not the ultimate objective of our congregation. We dare not say when the building is up, "Now we have completed our task." That would be to trust the building as an idol. The people of Israel did that with the first temple. Jeremiah rebuked the religious leaders of Israel when he stood in the gate of the first temple and said, "Do not trust in these deceptive words: 'This is the temple of the

Lord, the temple of the Lord, the temple of the Lord'" (Jer. 7:4 RSV). The people of Israel had believed that they were safe from the Babylonians—in spite of the moral degeneracy of their country—because the beautiful temple of Solomon stood in Jerusalem.

It is easy for us to have a false sense of values in material things, even though they are dedicated to God. Sir John Franklin, an English naval officer, led an expedition to the Canadian Arctic in 1845. His two ships and 104 men were lost. After more than 20 years of searching for the lost expedition, other explorers finally pieced together what happened. Most of Franklin's men died of exhaustion and starvation. One of the most ironic aspects of the death of Franklin and his men was that almost to the end they had been carrying a heavy load of silverware from the officers' mess. They had apparently valued tradition more than life itself.

A church building is meant to help sustain the life of the congregation—to bless people, to serve people, to help them learn the Word of God, and to help them have joy in Jesus Christ. As a youngster growing up in Washington, D. C., I recall our beautiful church building of Christ Lutheran Church. As young teenagers we were allowed to play touch football on the church lawn. Perhaps there were those who criticized us for this and thought we were ruining the beautiful lawn. But the pastor and church leaders permitted it. When the youth group met in the basement we all played hard, and I'm sure our eager play prematurely aged the chairs and tables. I do not advocate careless use of church property. But I say that we must never forget that the building and property are meant to be used, worn out, and expended in the service of the King, Jesus. If some glowering trustee had told us years ago to quit playing on the church lawn, or to sit quietly in the church basement, I wonder how I would have felt about the church. The church building is not an ultimate objective. The ultimate objective is to use the physical temple to build the spiritual temple!

The Spiritual Temple

Long ago, at the cornerstone laying of the second Jewish temple, Ezra, the high priest, led his people in praising God. Our text says, "they sang responsively, praising and giving thanks to the Lord, 'For He is good, for His steadfast love endures forever toward Israel' " (Ezra 3:11 RSV). The very heart of their praise and thanksgiving was their recollection of the "steadfast love" of God.

God has clearly and perfectly expressed His steadfast love toward the new Israel, the Christian church, in His Son, Jesus. And Jesus is the cornerstone of the spiritual temple, as Paul writes: "Christ Jesus Himself being the cornerstone, in which the whole structure is joined together and grows into a holy temple in the Lord; in whom you also are built into it for a dwelling place of God in the Spirit" (Eph. 2:20-22 RSV). Jesus is the cornerstone of the spiritual temple of God, and without Him the temple would collapse. The cornerstone of a building determines the alignment and placement of all the other stones in the building. The religion of Islam had its great prophet, Muhammed. Muhammed is dead, but Islam still exists as a religion because of its scriptures, the Koran. The Christian religion is different. If Jesus were not raised from the dead, our religion would be dead, and the whole Bible would be worse than useless. It would be a lie. The whole Bible points to Jesus. Peter writes: "For it stands in Scripture: 'Behold, I am laying in Zion a Stone, a Cornerstone chosen and precious, and he who believes in Him will not be put to shame' " (1 Peter 2:6 RSV). It was not just a good man who died on the cross on Golgotha. It was the Son of God, who could not remain dead, who now lives! His blood, death, and resurrection *qualify us* to be built into the spiritual temple of God. Without Christ, none of us, no matter how religious we think we are, is good enough to be used in God's spiritual temple. The Book of Revelation speaks of heaven and says "nothing unclean shall enter it, nor anyone who practices abomination or falsehood" (Rev. 21:27 RSV). God will have no imperfections in His temple. All mankind would be rejected, except for Jesus Christ. But in Him anyone can become a living stone in God's perfect spiritual temple.

Peter writes:

> Come to him, to that living stone, rejected by men but in God's sight chosen and precious; and like living stones be yourselves built into a spiritual house, to be a holy priesthood (1 Peter 2:4-5 RSV).

The materials used in any building are varied. There is concrete, plaster board, wood, stone, copper piping, tile—all fulfilling unique functions. Some materials, like the plumbing and wiring, are invisible in the final structure; others, like light fixtures or panelling, are highly visible. So it is with the spiritual temple of God. Each of us is unique, and has a unique function. The Holy Spirit in His wisdom gifts us all differently. Some Christians are gifted in the ability to render help—they are drawn to helping put on a church dinner or to assist with a maintenance project. Others have a gift of encouragement and, like Aaron and Hur of old, "hold up the hands" of the pastor and other leaders so they can continue their work. They are the ones who give the fitting word of praise and encouragement to the pastor when he is discouraged and ready to quit. We certainly must commend a builder for making a building out of more than wood! And we ought to praise God that he makes His spiritual temple out of different types of people, having differing gifts.

The people of Israel praised God with trumpets, cymbals, and responsive singing. We read in Psalm 150 that God was praised with trumpet, lute, harp, timbrel, strings, pipe, and cymbals.

Let us praise God with all our strength and with as many means as possible for this new physical temple. May it be in years to come a temple of praise! And let us praise God especially for the spiritual temple that He is building—his church—this congregation!

Christ is our Cornerstone	Oh, then, with hymns of praise
On Him alone we build;	These hallowed courts shall ring;
With His true saints alone	Our voices we will raise
The courts of heav'n are filled.	The Three in One to sing
On His great love	And thus proclaim
Our hopes we place	In joyful song,
Of present grace	Both loud and long,
And joys above	That glorious name. *(TLH* 465)

Come to Jesus, the living stone, and be built into Him and into His people! Amen.   Bruce J. Lieske

Related Scripture readings

Ex. 35:30-36:7;	Ps. 127:1a	Acts 4:11-12
cf. Ex. 31:1-11	Is. 28:16	Eph. 2:20-22
Neh. 2:18	Hag. 1:4-6, 12-14	1 Peter 2:4-5
Ps. 118:22-24	Zech. 4:7-9	

Suggested hymns

"The Church's One Foundation"
"Behold the Sure Foundation-Stone"
"Christ Is Our Cornerstone"
"Christ, Thou Art the Sure Foundation"
"Built on the Rock the Church Doth Stand"
"In the Name Which Earth and Heaven"
"O Lord of Hosts, Whose Glory Fills"

CHURCH DEDICATION

We See God Here Today

1 KINGS 8:27-30; IS. 6:1-7

It was a wonderful day—not unlike today!

Then—a beautiful new temple; now—a fine new house of God for worship.

Then there was gathered a dedication crowd of God's people. Today the same is said for us—we are God's people. We gather to celebrate His goodness.

Solomon's first words expressed praise to the Lord God of Israel. Before the altar Solomon prayed as the leader of his people. Our celebration began and continues with praise to Father, Son, and Holy Spirit. Before our God we rejoice today—each of us as a child of God, one of His family members.

Solomon asked "Can You, O God, really live on earth?" (1 Kings 8:27 TEV). We declare and confess: God, not only *can* You—but you *did*—in Jesus, Your Son, our Savior, and You still do through Your Spirit, who lives in each of us and has made our hearts Your temples.

Solomon stated: "The heavens can't contain You—much less this temple, which has been built." We echo that today: "You are great and magnificent, and this place can't contain You—and we didn't build it for that purpose."

The prayer then is still our prayer today! "Watch over this place, where You have chosen to be worshiped! Hear the prayers of Your people who come to praise *You* and hear *You* and hearing—forgive!" What a lovely word that is! That relationship, being the forgiven of God, makes us His own! We are His abode, His living temples, for the One whom even the heavens can't contain chooses in His grace to live in us by faith and among us in His Word and Sacraments. His precious means of grace assure us of the forgiveness won for us by Jesus our Savior. As His people we dedicate this place to His glory and for His worship and praise, and as a holy place where He through the means of His Grace can establish and strengthen faith in Him and love for Him. Isaiah was granted the vision. He was privileged to see God in the Temple erected to His glory! We are here today by His Spirit's leading, and we see God in this place—erected to His glory!

We See God Here Today

1. Here we see His greatness and majesty. Isaiah saw Him on His throne! He is King of kings and Lord of Lords!

He is high and lifted up, exalted and honored.

His robe filled the temple. He is all and in all!

Above the throne he saw the six-winged seraphim.

> With two wings they covered faces in humility.
> Even they can't look at that divine brilliance!
> With two they covered their feet and body.
> Even they are not worthy to stand before Him!
> With two they fly aloft! Their cry of praise is an extolling of the holiness of God.

"Holy, holy, holy! The Lord Almighty is holy!" (Is. 6:3a TEV).

It shouts to the world the universality of His rule!
    "His glory fills the world" (v. 36).
The temple shook and the smoke of holiness filled the place!

We, here today, see God. It is not the same vision, but yet it is a vision! God's Spirit lets us see, in the place we have built and in the Word that fills it, the vision of God's greatness! We are aware of His creative power. We see His preserving and His sustaining love. We hear the heavenly message of our holy God—and His claim to lordship and rule. He has made us, and not we ourselves. The whole world is in His hands. His majesty and His strength uphold all that He has made. He rules forever in the heavens as Lord. His glory fills the heavens and the earth. With Isaiah we extol His greatness and sing His praise: "Holy, holy, holy! Lord God Almighty! All Thy works shall praise Thy name in earth and sky and sea!" *(TLH* 264:4).

2. Here we find His forgiving grace. Isaiah's reaction is expected. He cries, "There is no hope for me. He's so great, so holy, and I'm so weak and evil! My lips are not pure and clean—and all around me is impurity and unrighteousness."

God gave Isaiah the blessedness of seeing a seraph take a coal from the altar—and touch it to his lips. The gracious words explain the unusual act! "Your guilt is gone and your sins are forgiven" (Is. 6:7 TEV).

God keeps telling us in Jesus Christ, "You are mine, forgiven and free! You are treasured and tenderly tended by the Good Shepherd. You are lavishly loved. You are clothed in royal, righteous raiment! You occupy the pecular position of being My own precious possession."

As we come to the place of His presence, we come with the same awareness of our sinfulness. We look into the mirror of God's law and see the image of imperfection peering back at us. We have failed to meet God's expectations for our lives. Those hateful words and loveless acts— the failure to speak when we had the chance—the lack of concern for those who needed help—words and deeds and thoughts that offended God and alienated us from Him and from one another! Truly we have unclean lips and live in a world of people with unclean lips. All of this prompts us to confess our guilt. We see God in His holiness and join Isaiah in saying: "Woe is me! For I am lost!" (Is. 6:5 RSV).

But we see not only our guilt. Here today and every day we see God in His forgiving grace toward us in Jesus Christ. We see the cross and remember His sacrifice for our sins. We see the altar and remember that His body and blood were given and shed for us for our forgiveness. We see the font and remember the covenant through the water and the word and the power of His Spirit. We see the pulpit and remember that God speaks through His word telling us that in Jesus Christ He has reconciled us to Himself. His good news is that our sins were on Jesus—and He died and was buried and rose again, that God's mercy could be ours and that Christ's life and love might likewise be ours.

3. Here we hear His call to service. Isaiah heard God's call that day in the temple. "Whom shall I send? Who will be our messenger?" (Is. 6:8 TEV).

It was a call to service. And Isaiah answered it! The experience was so real—the excitement so intense—the impact so powerful, that God's forgiveness moved Isaiah's response of yielding himself to God: "Here I am, Lord. I'm yours! Take me and use me."

Again and again the call is heard, in this place and wherever it is that our God desires to speak to us. His strong Word that cleaved the darkness and brought forth light, still comes to us in the recital of the great acts for our salvation. He does His transforming work in us through His Spirit. He is a sending Lord! He has a mission for us! He creates us—saves us—cleanses us—forgives us—adopts us—empowers us, so that we may be His spokesmen, His representatives.

In the days and years ahead, most especially in this place set apart for your worship and adoration, God will time and again reveal His love and issue His call! It will come to experienced elder servants of His, with long years of faithful discipleship, and it will come to the newly won for Christ's kingdom. It will come to busy businessmen and to housewives preoccupied with family chores. It will come to young men and women busily preparing for a career—or to laborers and office workers, teachers and lawyers, nurses and clerks. It is His call to lives that reflect His forgiving Love. It is His call to service form Him.

It isn't always a call to the heroic! It often involves the insignificant, the unnoticed little things! It is a call for faithfulness to principle and moral precepts in the thousands of decisions that need to be made each day—to integrity and uprightness—when seemingly no one was looking, and no one could know—but God! It is a call to compassion and concern for the needy and the neglected, for the lonely and oppressed, for those who just need a friend—a kindly smile, a word of hope, a prayer for strength.

The sending Lord looks for those who will go out for Him! Discipleship is not always just following wherever the pathway leads, but going instead where there is no path and blazing a new trail in uncharted territory! His call asks us to venture out, not playing it safe by sailing close to shore and safe harbor, but risking ourselves far out on the sea of life, away from the lights of land, to the place where the stars shine brilliantly and the only source of guidance must come from Someone other than self.

To You, holy God, we dedicate this house. Help us always to see You here in Your majesty and glory, in the forgiving love You have for us in Jesus Christ, and in the call which You give us again and again to serve

You as Your people. Live here, O God, and live in us that we may live under You in Your kingdom and reflect Your greatness and Your love to the people of Your world. Amen.   Lloyd Behnken

Related Scripture readings

John 8:30-36   Ex. 40:17-38

Suggested hymns

"Isaiah, Mighty Seer, in Days of Old"
"Holy, Holy, Holy! Lord God Almighty!"
"Great Is the Lord, Our God"
"The Church's One Foundation"
"Zion, Rise, Zion, Rise"

EVANGELISM

How to Be a Gospel Runner

ACTS 8:1-4

Play a "word association game" with me, will you? What is the first thing that comes to your mind when you hear the word "evangelism"? There are few words in our common vocabulary that bring as many different associations. Are some of yours like the ones I have heard from others?

Elmer Gantry
Billy Sunday
Billy Graham
The movie *Marjoe*
Two Mormons visiting house-to-house on our street.
Two ladies from the Jehovah's witnesses visiting us.
Moonies selling flowers.
Hare Krishna followers chanting on a street corner

I guess we could go on and on, and you could add more associations, but some are more in the Lutheran context, like:

The Lutheran Hour—or Dr. Oswald Hoffmann
Key 73—or Dr. Ted Raedeke
Our Evangelism Committee
The Wednesday night callers who visit new people

Now, all these associations are not really wrong, but they are incomplete. Today as we focus our attention on evangelism in this service, we want to get at the very heart of the meaning of the word and give it a focus that involves all of us. We have chosen a text from the Bible that uses the word evangelism, at least in the original New Testament Greek—and make our theme: "How to be a Gospel Runner." We will explain that theme as we consider three things necessary to be a Gospel Runner: Have the Gospel; tell the Gospel; do it with my special gifts.

I. Have the Gospel

The text is from the history of the early church, right after the death of Stephen, the first martyr. As he was stoned, a devout young Pharisee named Saul watched over the clothes of the stoners, in full agreement with the action, so much so that he became involved in the severe persecution of the early Christians in Jerusalem. He "was ravaging the church, and entering house after house, he dragged off men and women and committed them to prison" (Acts 8:3 RSV). This later led to Saul's going to Damascus to persecute the Christians there, and that led to his conversion on the road there.

But today we are concerned in this text with what the people did who were being persecuted. When the "great persecution arose against the church . . . they were all scattered throughout the region of Judea, and Samaria, except the apostles" (Acts 8:1 RSV). The apostles felt it their duty to stay and care for the people who remained in Jerusalem and to continue the outreach of the church there. It was the lay people—men, women, and children—who sold their possessions and moved to the next state, Judea, and to the next, Samaria. It was these lay men, women, and children of whom Luke then writes: "those who were scattered went about preaching the Word" (Acts 8:4 RSV). A little phrase—"went about preaching the Word." I really don't like that translation, although I like what it says. The Greek word translated "preach" does not carry the same meaning as our English word "preach." When you first hear that verse, you think of someone standing in a pulpit or on a platform and preaching a sermon, don't you? And you think of a preacher doing it. That is not what happened. These are lay men, women, and children who are doing the preaching, and their preaching is done wherever they are, by talking to whoever they have a chance to—their neighbors, the workers at their side, the traveler on the road, the lady washing her clothes in the lake or getting water from the well. One commentator said it was like "gossiping" the Gospel in all their talk. The Greek word used here and translated "preach" is *euangellizomai*. It was used in the Greek language long before the New Testament was written.

One example of how the Greek word was used comes from Greek history. In the year 490 B. C. a small army of Athenians fought a much larger army from Persia on the plains near the city of Marathon in the province of Attica, Greece. The expertise and devotion of soldiers from Athens won the day in an amazing victory. The Greeks chose one of their fastest runners and sent him to Athens to tell the good news. He ran all the way, shouted to the city "Rejoice, we have won," and then fell over dead from his overexertion. When Greek historians recorded this incident, they used that word—*euangellizomai.*

The Holy Spirit put into the mind of the New Testament writers that word for "tell good news" about Jesus Christ and the related word *euanggelion* for the noun "good news"—as when the angel Gabriel came to Zechariah to bring him "good news" (Luke 1:19 RSV) and when the angel told the shepherds, "I bring you good news of great joy" (Luke 2:10 RSV). Long ago the English word for "good" was "god," and the words for "news" was "spell." The two together made the word "godspell," or, as we have it today, "Gospel." The lay people in the text brought good news wherever they went.

What is the Good News—the Gospel—with which we are to run into all the world? The Gospel comes from God. He sent the angel to tell it, and He sent His Son to accomplish it because of His love (John 3:16). It is good news, because it comes from God and tells us how to be saved. It is not good news, however, for those who do not know the bad news—the bad news that they need saving. If I don't know I'm sick, I won't feel the need for a doctor. The bad news was summed up by Jesus very sharply one day in speaking to the Pharisees. He said, "If you believe not that I am He, you will die in your sins" (John 8:24). He was saying two things: first, that they were sinners; second, that because of their sins, they would die—be eternally separated from God. That was the bad news. The good news is that Jesus came to take our sin upon Himself and die in our place to pay the penalty of sin. It's good news to know that because of the death and resurrection of Jesus, I have forgiveness and new life, a full and meaningful life, here and now, and the assurance of an eternity of bliss with God in heaven.

A man lay in a hospital bed waiting for the report from the lab of the biopsy that was to show if his tumor was malignant or benign. He thought: There can be two answers. Either the doctor is going to say, "the tumor is malignant. It will do no good to operate. You have about six months, and then you'll die." Or the good news could be, "the tumor is benign. We'll remove it, and you'll be as good as new in six weeks." When the doctor finally came he said, "It's benign. After an operation, you'll be as good as new in six weeks." That was good news, because he knew what the bad news might have been.

Only in our case, we all start with cancer—the cancer of sin. We are all dying and headed to an eternity in hell. The good news is: Look to Jesus, be healed, and you will live forever. Jesus wants you to share this Good News with others. Can you imagine having a cure for cancer and not sharing it with your relative or friend who is dying of cancer? We have the Good News—the Gospel.

II. Tell the Gospel

The text uses the English word "preach" for telling that Gospel. The Athenian runner probably shouted his good news of victory. Those lay men, women, and children in Judea and Samaria told their Good News, the victory of the risen Lord, in normal, everyday conversation. Another word that some people use today is "share"—"share" the Gospel. "Share" carries with it the idea that I have something I want you to have, as when I want to share with you a piece of bread or a refreshing drink. The important thing is that we tell the story—the story of Jesus' death and resurrection. But not only do we tell the Gospel, we also live the Gospel. This is what is sometimes called preparation for telling the Gospel, or "pre-evangelism." Like a farmer plows and discs the soil before he sows the seeds, so our living the Gospel, our being as Jesus said, the salt of the earth and the light of the world (Matt. 5:13-14), is the plowing and discing that prepares hearts to receive the Gospel seed that we sow. The sowing itself is what we say. We are, as Jesus said, His witnesses (Acts 1:8 RSV). We tell what we have "heard and seen" (Luke 2:20), what we have experienced, what the Gospel means in our lives, as well as what the Scriptures tell about it.

III. Do It with Special Gifts

How to be a Gospel Runner? Have the Gospel and share it. How? That is our third point. Do it with the special gifts that God has given to you. The New Testament teaches that every Christian is given a spiritual gift or gifts (1 Cor. 12:7; Romans 12:6; 1 Peter 4:10) to use for the health and growth of the church, the body of Christ. Some have the special gift of evangelism—of telling the Gospel to special effect. There was an office of evangelist, just like there was the office of apostle and pastor and teacher, in the early church. But lay people also had the gift of evangelism. One of the first deacons, Philip, is called an evangelist. He shared the Gospel and many believed through his witness. Today in congregations that emphasize training people to make regular evangelism calls, the experience is that about 10 percent of an average congregation seems to have this special gift. They are marathon Gospel runners.

The marathon race is named after Marathon, Greece, where the battle that we mentioned earlier was fought. The distance for a marathon race is about 26 miles because that was perhaps about the distance from Marathon to Athens. But not all of us are marathoners. Some of us can run only a mile or two and some of us can only walk fast. But all of us are "runners" in the sense that we move from one place to another. It is as we move, either as marathoners or walkers, that we carry the Gospel and share it with whomever we meet on the way. We can describe it by saying that we all are witnesses, and some of us have the special gift of being evangelists.

Whichever it is for you, all of us need to be using the special gifts that God has given to us to spread the Gospel. C. Peter Wagner, leader in the American Church Growth Movement, calls the gift of evangelist the primary organ in the body of Christ for adding new members of the church. But all the other organs of the body should also function properly. All of us need to use our spiritual gifts—gifts of teaching, serving, giving, teaching, leadership, administration, mercy, or whatever it may be.

A pastor preached a powerful sermon one Sunday on how everyone in the church ought to be doing his share of the work. At the door that morning a little old lady, Mrs. Smith, commented very sincerely, "I'd like to do my part, but there is nothing I can do." And she may have been right in terms of teaching Sunday school, leading in some organization of the church, or singing in the choir. The comment bothered the pastor until an idea came to him. He called Mrs. Smith later that day and said, "I know something you can do. You know that family down the block from you, the Blacks? Mrs. Black is in the hospital and Mr. Black is trying to care for the children himself. Why don't you see if you can be of some help." Here was something she could do. She baked her best apple strudel, took it over, and offered a helping hand. The pastor remembered and called her again and again. Soon other members were calling her whenever some new family came to town or someone was in need. And soon Mrs. Smith could add her witness to her serving. When someone would say, "Why do you do this for us?" She could say, "Because I love Jesus and I love you." Mrs. Smith was a Gospel runner, using the gifts God had given her. She carried the Gospel and shared it.

The word "evangel" is made up of "ev" and "angel." An angel, in the meaning of the Greek word, is a messenger. "Ev" in Greek means good. God used angels to be his messengers, his Gospel runners. They came to Zechariah, to Mary, to Joseph, and to the shepherds. They came at Easter with the message, "He is risen. He is alive." Today God does not send His angels to be His Gospel runners. The angels watch over the runners and protect them, but the runners are you and me, the ones who have the Gospel, who know and love Jesus as Savior and Lord. Amen.

Erwin J. Kolb

Related Scripture readings

Matt. 28:19-20   2 Cor. 5:16-21   Acts 1:6-11   Matt. 10:32-33

Suggested hymns

"Onward, Christian Soldiers"
"Stand Up, Stand Up for Jesus"
"Hark! the Voice of Jesus Crying"
"Soldiers of the Cross, Arise"
"Spread, Oh, Spread, Thou Mighty Word"
"There Still Is Room"

FUNERAL

The Christian's Confidence

PS. 27:1-4

Remembering your loved one, and being anxious to have a word from our Lord that we can cling to, that can fill our emptiness, we invite you now to note this word in Psalm 27:1-4 (KJV): "The Lord is my Light and my Salvation; whom shall I fear? the Lord is the Strength of my life; of whom shall I be afraid? When the wicked, even mine enemies and my foes, came upon me to eat up my flesh, they stumbled and fell. Though a host should encamp against me, my heart shall not fear: though war should rise against me, in this will I be confident. One thing have I desired of the Lord, that will I seek after; that I may dwell in the house of the Lord all the days of my life, to behold the beauty of the Lord, and to inquire in His temple."

This is one of my favorite passages, because it is one of many that have much meaning for shut-ins—those who by reason of years or health are unable to mingle with others as they formerly did—those to whom we must minister privately. A passage like this lifts them and meets them in their need. Today, you are seeking to draw from the Word of the Lord strength and meaning that will enable you to look ahead and realize that there is more to life than just this hour of death.

As we approach this Word, we also keep in mind that you experienced a particular kind of frustration these last weeks. You wanted to share some thoughts with your dear mother; particularly the thought that her husband had died. You wanted to be able to share that with her in order to offer her strength and support. This was terribly frustrating, because you knew you couldn't do that. Each day you looked for a new opportunity; but of course it didn't happen. She could not understand. In the wisdom of the Lord, now we see that it is far better that way. That particular kind of anguish, that particular kind of loss and need she was spared. The kind of frustration you felt is a mark on life here. Many things frustrate, trouble, and distress us. That is why this particular passage is so very meaningful. In the middle of all of the disruption of life here, the trying times in which the world is just now, in the midst of all of this, we can think about

The Christian's Confidence

I. Its Foundation

Knowledge

What do these verses tell us about the foundation for this confidence? Listen again. "The Lord is my Light and my Salvation; whom shall I fear? the Lord is the Strength of my life; of whom shall I be afraid?" Immediately you see the foundation for real confidence. It is found in knowledge. That sounds like the philosophy that is so strong in our day. If you have the right knowledge, you can get along. Please note immediately, this knowledge is different. This is a heaven-given knowledge. This is the knowledge that has to do with the soul's well-being. This is the knowledge that says, "When I think about God, I know that He is my Light." What a picture that is!

[Light

You have noticed that the church and chapel are different compared to three weeks ago. The signs of the Festival of Light, of Christmas, are all around. Those lights all stem from the realization that in the Lord Jesus we really have the Light of the world.]

Salvation

You remember that your loved one knew from God's Holy Word that the Lord was indeed the Light of her life. Because she knew Him as her precious Savior, there could be light in her life and there could be hope and confidence. First, there was the knowledge that God is light. Then there was the knowledge that "God is my Salvation." That is the basis for confidence. Salvation—what a precious, beautiful truth—the gateway to eternity opened wide—the recognition that I am not lost, not left hopeless in the gloom—my Lord invites me to note that I am His child forever. How beautiful that your dear one could know this and could share it with you, just as she did with her husband.

Strength

And there is the knowledge that "God is my Strength." All of these are words that have meaning for each one of us. When we use the word "strength," we all have our own picture of it in mind. We are often filled with the realization that we need a source of strength. We are up against something that we don't know how to take anymore. We need strength. We understand what it is to have somebody give us what we need. We understand what it is to have somebody take hold of a job and help get it done; to have somebody come and be with us just when we need it most; to have somebody share one little word that lets us know we are not in this alone. To be able to say, "God is my Strength," is a precious confidence to have. That really is the basis for the Christian's confidence. What does that make possible? It makes possible saying, "What have I to fear? What am I afraid of?" It makes possible being absolutely free of fear and saying, "I am completely in God's care." You remember your dear one and her confidence. She could say, "God is my Light and my Salvation and my Strength."

II. Its Contents

The Christian's confidence—what does it do? What is its contents? "One thing have I desired of the Lord, that will I seek after; that I may dwell in the house of the Lord all the days of my life, to behold the beauty of the Lord, and to inquire in His temple." Can't you visualize a prayer like that by your loved one? That is the content of the Christian's confidence.

"The House of the Lord"

The Christian says: "That I may dwell in the house of the Lord." Many things fit into that phrase. We speak of a place like this chapel as the house of the Lord. Can you think of anything that a real child of God, who loves the Word of the Lord and who wants to praise and honor His name, could desire more than being in God's house, day by day, hearing His word, praying together with other believers, and singing His praises? That is one picture of the "house of the Lord."

You remember that, when it was possible for her, your loved one regularly and eagerly went to such a "house of the Lord."

But there is more. To be in the house of the Lord also means to be in God's family, to be His child by faith in Jesus the Savior. And what would a real child of God desire more than to be in the family of God? That's what the Christian's confidence is.

And there is still another picture. The house of the Lord is also heaven, the eternal home. What is there for a child of God to desire more than to be at home forever with the heavenly Father? That is made possible because the Lord Jesus came into the world as a little baby at Christmastime. Before His mission was completed he had been on the cross, and in the tomb, and had risen again. All of this is the heart of our Christian faith. Your mother confessed this faith. She could say: "One thing have I desired . . . that I may dwell in the house of the Lord all the days of my life, to behold the beauty of the Lord." Isn't that an inviting thought?

"The Beauty of the Lord"

[The beauty of God is seen in the Christmas tree, the Christmas lights, and the Christmas message: "I bring you good tidings of great joy . . . for unto you is born this day in the city of David a Savior, which is Christ the Lord" (Luke 2:10-11 KJV).] The beauty of God is seen in His message of love and forgiveness. It was often your dear one's privilege to hear that message of God, "You are forgiven. Be at peace." Her heart thrilled to the beauty of God.

"Inquire in His Temple"

". . . to inquire in His temple." That is a great picture, too. The child of God is eager to inquire, to ask of God wisdom, understanding, and guidance and direction for life. We face sober decisions. Where do we turn, but to God? We say, "Lord, I don't know how to go on. Show me the way. Show me what is right." It was your mother's privilege, as a believer in Jesus Christ, to inquire in His temple, to see the great truth of His Word.

That is the content of the Christian's confidence. Our Lord invites you to have it in your heart. We invite you to share with each other this Word as you recount the many memories of events long ago, or recently, when you gathered to celebrate anniversaries or birthdays. The memories you will talk about will have a blessed meaning as you undergird them with the words of Psalm 27:1-4. You will say: "Thank God for Christian confidence!" Amen.   Ernest L. Gerike

Related Scripture readings

1 Peter 1:3-9	Jer. 17:7-8	Ps. 39:7-13
1 John 3:18-24	Ps. 1	Ps. 146
1 John 5:9-15	Ps. 16:7-11	Rom. 12:9-18
Eph. 3:8-12		

Suggested hymns

"My Hope Is Built On Nothing Less"
"Jesus, Thy Blood and Righteousness"
"Come Unto Me, Ye Weary"
"Jesus, Thy Boundless Love to Me"
"My Faith Looks Up to Thee"

CHURCH GROUNDBREAKING

The Good Way: The Right Way

1 SAM. 12:23-24

At a time of great decision, Samuel told God's people long ago to rededicate themselves to their Lord, remembering the great things He had done for them. As this congregation today assembles on this property, set aside for the Gospel ministry, and by the rite of ground-breaking initiates the building of its first unit, the Scripture calls: "Fear the Lord, and serve Him in truth with all your heart" (KJV).

These are days of important decision for your congregation. You have reached agreement on a plan for the physical structure that is to rise on this site. The beauty of this building, its functional qualities for present service, and its adaptability to a future expanded program were achieved after many hours of prayerful study, intense effort, and many lengthy conferences. You are now committed by contract to this building project; your major questions have been resolved.

But you are at the same time developing another structure that requires many important, and often difficult, decisions. You are formulating the structure of your congregation and its program and life. Today, and in all of your tomorrows, the decisions you make regarding this soul-building and congregation-building program will be all-important. Although in your constitution you have laid the broad base on which you will structure your joint worship activities and your cooperative service, you will constantly have to restudy and reshape your plans and your programs to meet the changing and growing opportunities that the Lord lays before you.

In the building of the Lord's kingdom, the personnel and the program are both more important than the property that houses them, as St. Paul pointed out in Eph. 2:19-22 (KJV): "Ye are no more strangers and foreigners, but fellow citizens with the saints, and of the household of God; and are built upon the foundation of the apostles and prophets, Jesus Christ Himself being the chief Cornerstone; in whom all the building fitly framed together groweth unto an holy temple in the Lord: in whom ye also are builded together for an habitation of God through the Spirit."

These are challenging and decisive days for all of us assembled here in the Lord's name. By God's gracious choice we have been individually called to faith and to new life in Jesus Christ, and we have been placed in a position of great leadership and influence. The Word of the Lord reminds us: "He died for all, that they which live should not henceforth live unto themselves, but unto Him which died for them and rose again" (2 Cor. 5:15 KJV). The same Lord who said: "Because I live, ye shall live also" (John 14:19 KJV), pointed to the world of men who live outside the realm of forgiven sins and said: "As My Father hath sent Me, even so send I you" (John 20:21 KJV). We are becoming more and more aware that the harvest truly is plenteous, but the laborers are few. We recognize the necessity of impressing on individual hearts and individual members of the church that special mission which the Lord, after He called them to forgiveness and peace in Himself, assigned them in this world: that they might be witnesses of His victory and of God's holy purpose among men, that by their offering of themselves and of their resources to the Savior's service, they might be used by the Spirit of God in building and extending the walls of God's kingdom.

As we enter each new day, we are impressed by the simple lesson that the clocks teach us. As one day ends and a new one begins, the clocks raise both of their hands toward heaven. So ought we, as we pass from one phase of the church's life into another! As we enter each new day's work for the Lord, we ought to point our hands toward heaven—in thanksgiving for the blessings we have known and in supplication for the blessings we require for life and service, owning God as the Strength of our life and our sure Help forever.

The prophet Samuel gave similar advice to God's people long ago when they found themselves in changing times. We do well to hear and to ponder his words again today: "I will teach you the good and the right way: only fear the Lord, and serve Him in truth with all your heart: for consider how great things He hath done for you" (1 Sam. 12:23-24 KJV).

As we carry out the responsibilities of our various offices and callings in life, as each of us moves forward in our own way in the ventures of faith to which God invites us, there will undoubtedly be many variations in our approach to and in our application of this directive to the specific situations that greet us. But there ought to be a basic unity about all that we do, as the Lord advises us in the text.

The prophet said: "Only fear the Lord." Certainly we have cause for reverential fear as we view the infirmities of our life and the record of failures that we bring to the task before us. We are deeply humbled by the privileged position in which we find ourselves: God's witnesses in our society, declarers of His glory and voices of the Gospel's invitation. But God does not intend that we should let feelings of awe or any sense of unworthiness deter us from confronting the opportunities He gives. "My grace is sufficient for you," He tells us, "for My strength is made perfect in weakness." We do not walk alone, we do not work alone. With the great apostle Paul, we have learned to say: "I live; yet not I, but Christ liveth in me; and the life which I now live in the flesh I live by the faith of the Son of God, who loved me and gave Himself for me" (Gal. 2:20 KJV).

"Only fear the Lord." What holy awe fills our hearts as we ponder the working of God! That same Spirit of God who brought us to faith in Christ and taught us to clasp the forgiveness of life and peace that are Christ's gifts to us now works in our hearts to build the joy of our response in our new life with God. The apostle speaks to us as he called to Christians long ago: "Know ye not that your body is the temple of the Holy Ghost, which is in you, which ye have of God, and ye are not your own? For ye are bought with a price: therefore glorify God in your body and in your spirit, which are God's" (1 Cor. 6:19-20 KJV).

"Only fear the Lord." God calls for a holy reverence in us that will teach us to build a continuing consciousness of our dependence upon Him. He wants us to experience the thrill and the growth in grace that comes from faithful study of His Word; He wants us to discover the majesty of fervent daily prayer; He wants us to tremble with grateful astonishment as we see the beauty of His gifts unfolding in our hearts and lives. That calls us to reconsider each day the promise of our relationship to Him, the splendor of His never-changing character, the experience of the vibrant goodness of His saving and soul-strengthening purpose in our life.

Then it will follow that we will "serve Him in truth with all our heart." Here is the loving echo of another passage: "Thou shalt worship the Lord, Thy God, and Him only shalt thou serve "(Matt. 4:10 KJV). The word of Law that we could not keep becomes an invitation of grace as the Spirit of God moves in our hearts. We hear the heroic apostle saying: "By the grace of God I am what I am: and His grace which was bestowed upon me was not in vain; but I laboured more abundantly than they all: yet not I, but the grace of God which was with me" (1 Cor. 15:10 KJV).

Faith calls us to service; and here is the good way, the right way: a sincere and wholehearted offering of ourselves to the life and labor we share in the Lord. This is not service dictated by our whim, by our likes or dislikes, but by our surrendered heart's cry: "Lord, what wilt Thou have me to do?" (Acts 9:6 KJV). John Ruskin wrote: "He who offers God a second place offers Him no place." The good and the right way forbids catering to ourselves by choosing the easy way; it prevents coddling of our coworkers or compromise to the standards of our day. It requires and accomplishes a program of service that is patterned according to the divine will and to the Spirit's power, wholly dedicated to God's glory and to the advancement of His kingdom.

"Only" this, the text says. His "is the kingdom, and the power, and the glory" (Matt. 6:13 KJV). His is the mission, His the might, and His the majesty of accomplishment. The Lord does not ask us to respond with any resource that He Himself has not first entrusted to us; He does not ask us to respond to any opportunity that He Himself has not presented to us; He asks us for no measure of success than that to which His grace leads us. "It is required in stewards," Paul said, "that a man be found faithful" (1 Cor. 4:2 KJV). The Lord does not even say that we must succeed, He simply calls us lovingly to service.

"For consider how great things He hath done for you." In this text the Lord issues a call to genuine gratitude and to the happy motivation of confidence in our work. Because we know God's love, because we have experienced its power in our own heart and life, and because we rejoice in the continuation of God's mercy and might in all that we do, we labor cheerfully and with eagerness. Because we know Him as an unchanging God, we trust that He will crown our efforts with His blessing. Our labor is "not in vain in the Lord" (1 Cor. 15:58 KJV). We can do all things through Christ, who strengthens us (cf. Phil. 4:13).

As we give ourselves and our service to the Lord, we will hear the echo of the ancient promise: "Prove Me now herewith, saith the Lord of hosts, if I will not open you the windows of heaven, and pour you out a blessing, that there shall not be room enough to receive it" (Mal. 3:10 KJV).

May God fill our hearts with such devotion and such eagerness for service throughout the days of this special project and teach us through all time to come to stretch our hands upward to heaven—upward to the victory that God has won for us and for all mankind—upward to claim His blessing—and upward to offer ourselves to His purposes and His glory, for Jesus' sake. Amen.   Paul Ph. Spitz

Scripture readings

Rom. 12:1-7   Eph. 1:15-23   John 15:1-8

Suggested hymns

"Come, Holy Ghost, God and Lord"
"Come, Let Us Join Our Cheerful Songs"
"Come, Thou Almighty King"
"Jesus Calls Us; o'er the Tumult"
"Lord Jesus, Thou the Church's Head"
"Soul, What Return Has God, Thy Savior"

INSTALLATION OF A TEACHER

A Spiritual Training Program

2 TIM. 2:1-7

This is a very special day in your life and in the history of this congregation. It is a special day because it represents the culmination of much praying, planning, and congregational activity in calling a full-time worker to come and serve here. Whenever a Christian congregation issues a call in the name of the triune God to a person to come and promote the gospel of Jesus Christ among them—that is a red letter day in the life of a congregation. Whether that call is a call to a preaching minister to come and preach the Gospel and administer the sacraments and serve as a shepherd of the whole flock or whether, as in your case, it is a call to a teaching minister to come and teach the Word especially to children and to administer a program of Christian education, we know that it is a call from God through His people to do His work.

It is a day of rejoicing for both the congregation and the candidate. The congregation rejoices to know that the teacher whom God has led them to call has also been moved by the Holy Spirit to accept the call. It is a day of rejoicing for the teacher to be officially installed into the congregation's teaching ministry and to have the appropriate District representative acknowledge publicly by this ceremony the fitness of the candidate for this important position in the church.

God's Word speaks to those who are called to be professional servants of the church, such as pastors, teachers, and evangelists. That Word gives them some specific advice, instruction, and counsel. It is profitable for the whole congregation to listen carefully to what God's Word says to the called professional ministers. For, as we see what God expects of them, it enables us as members of a congregation to learn to know our roles and responsibilities more clearly, so that we may more effectively support and work with our called servants as co-laborers in the work of the church.

That some individuals in Christ's kingdom are called by God to serve in special capacities in His church as pastors or teachers or in other offices is self-evident as one reads the New Testament. The New Testament explicitly teaches that not every one in the church will occupy these positions. "Are all apostles? . . . are all teachers?" St. Paul asked the

Corinthians (1 Cor. 12:29 KJV). Of course not. If all were preachers or teachers then where were the hearers?

To those whom God leads into these specialized ministries of the Word, He also in His wisdom gives specific guidelines. Our text is an example of such clear directive advice, written by St. Paul, under the guidance and inspiration of the Holy Spirit, to Timothy, who was in the process of growing into a larger sphere of activity and responsibility in his ministry. Our text supplies us with a series of specific admonitions and directions, or training rules, for servants of God to follow, if they are to carry out ministry effectively and successfully. Let us consider this text under the theme,

A Spiritual Training Program
I. Be Strengthened in the Grace of Christ Jesus

St. Paul presents three specific words of advice to Timothy in this text, and they are especially fitting to you as a teaching minister. The first of these is by far the most important one. It is basic and fundamental. It is the foundation on which all subsequent directives must rest. That basic advice is this, "Be strong in the grace that is in Christ Jesus" (2 Tim. 2:1 KJV). More precisely translated, the text says, "Be *strengthened* in the grace that is in Christ Jesus." That is to be the source of your strength and your power for ministry: the grace of God that is in Christ Jesus. And what is that grace? It is the undeserved love and mercy of God for all sinful people of the world, including you and me.

It is the good news, the amazing, well-nigh unbelievable news that God, the righteous One, is looking down on all His creatures with compassion and pity and is offering them forgiveness of sins through Jesus Christ, His Son, who has died for them. It is God not imputing their trespasses to them, but laying all the sins of the world on Jesus and accepting His sacrifice, His suffering and death as full atonement. In that fact, and in the proclamation of that truth there is power and strength—strength for your personal life, strength for your spiritual life, and power for your ministry. St. Paul said it another way in Rom. 1:16, when he wrote, "I am not ashamed of the Gospel of Christ: for it is the power of God unto salvation to everyone that believeth" (KJV).

If you try to build your teaching ministry on anything else, other than the grace of God in Christ Jesus, you are wasting your time and your pupils' time. For "other foundation can no man lay than that is laid, which is Jesus Christ" (1 Cor. 3:11 KJV).

But there is always the temptation to seek power and strength in more spectacular devices and to look for more dramatic means than God has given us in His Word. Elijah the prophet looked for God in the raging wind and in the thundering earthquake, but the Lord was not there. Then he sought Him in the roaring fire, but God was not there. Finally came the still small voice, and God was there. God chooses to clothe His majestic grace in humility and lowliness. His still small voice still speaks quietly to us through His written Word. The wise men from the East sought the new born King in a palace, in a metropolis, only to discover Him in a rural area, in swaddling clothes, lying in a manger. God's truth does not need fanfare, or spectacular presentation to be effective.

God's grace still comes to people as a free gift, quietly and unobtrusively, as is so well expressed in the well-known Christmas carol.

> How silently, how silently, the wondrous Gift is giv'n!
> So God imparts To human hearts The blessings of His heav'n.
> No ear may hear His coming, But in this world of sin,
> Where meek souls will Receive Him still,
> The dear Christ enters in. *(TLH* 647:3)

Your task, boiled down to its simplest terms, is to rely and trust in that grace for yourself and to be strengthened by it. Then, following the example of John the Baptist, point your children in the classroom, and all whom you teach, to Him who is the very grace of God personified, saying, "Behold, the Lamb of God, who takes away the sin of the world!" (John 1:29 RSV). Relying solely on the grace of God for yourself and your ministry, your prime task and the responsibility to which you are called is to point your students to Jesus Christ as their only Lord, Savior, and King.

II. Be an Enabler

The second training rule is this, "Don't try to do it all yourself." Listen to what St. Paul writes in the text: "What you have heard from me before many witnesses entrust to faithful men who will be able to teach others also" (2 Tim. 2:2 RSV). You are not expected to create a new and original message. Rather you are to teach and transmit to others what you have been taught from God's Word. You are to commit to others the same Good News that has been transmitted to you. As God has used others to call you by the Gospel, you now have the high privilege to be God's agent in calling others by that same Gospel.

The task of the professional teaching and preaching ministries is to be sharers and enablers: ministers who enable people to be in ministry to one another. St. Paul here is saying "Remember what you heard from me and transmit that same content, that same doctrine, to others, to faithful people who will be able in turn to teach and tell others." Parents need to be equipped to teach and guide their children more effectively into the Word of God. Members of the congregation need to be equipped to teach Sunday school and vacation Bible school. Bible class leaders are needed. Elders and deacons are needed to visit the sick. Mission committees and evangelism committees are needed to plan, train, and equip the membership to do the work that Christ has given the whole church to do: to be in ministry to the whole world. The task of the full-time called pastor or teacher is to transmit the doctrine—the holy Word—that they have learned and help others to communicate to still others. You have received specialized training in education, psychology, and methods of teaching. You have studied the Word of God in depth in your theology classes at a Lutheran college. You are now also to share what you have learned and help others to learn to communicate that Word.

You are part of a team ministry. As a good team member you will want to support, encourage, and pray for every other member of this congregation's team: your pastor, your fellow teachers, your principal, and all supporting staff members. Moreover you must also remember to pray regularly for your pupils. God entrusts them to your care and spiritual nurture, but He reminds us that they are His lambs and His sheep. Prayer is a part of your spiritual training program. It must be done with regularity and faithfulness. Pray for your whole congregation and for the whole church in its mission of proclaiming and teaching the Gospel of Jesus Christ.

III. Anticipate Some Suffering for Christ's Sake

St. Paul's third piece of advice for your spiritual training program is this: "Take your share of suffering as a good soldier of Christ Jesus (cf. 2 Tim. 2:2). This is a word of caution applicable to every teacher of the Word of God. Be prepared to accept your share of suffering in the ministry of the Word. It is not the world's easiest job. It is not always "a bed of roses." Sometimes your best efforts will be misunderstood and criticized, not only by those outside the church, but even by those in the church.

Because you represent a holy God, some people will expect of you near perfection in your work. Some will forget from time to time that you are just as human as they are—subject to all the same temptations and perhaps to a few more that come uniquely to people who serve the church in full-time ministries. It is interesting to note that the word "soldier" appears several times in this chapter. A soldier is a warrior, one who wages war. He is engaged in combat. Every pastor and teacher is engaged in a never-ending battle with sin: with the devil, the world, and his own flesh. Verse 4 reminds you as a soldier not to get "entangled in civilian pursuits" (RSV). Your job is a full-time job. You are to devote yourself to it with singleness of purpose. The congregation should provide you with sufficient salary, so that it will not be necessary for you to engage in other work or enterprises in order to help feed and clothe yourself and your family. Neither are you to get overly involved in many extracurricular pursuits to the point at which it begins to diminish your effectiveness as a teaching minister and as a soldier of the cross.

IV. Work According to the Rules

Our text gives two closing illustrations to show the importance of a good spiritual training program. Verse 5 says, "An athlete is not crowned unless he competes according to the rules" (RSV). St. Paul must have been an avid sports fan in his day. So often he draws on the world of sports for illustrations. God's servants must play their roles according to the rules. They are not exempt from God's standards of Christian behavior. You can never say as a Christian teacher, "Do as I say but not as I do." One who would teach the law of love must live the law of love first in their own life. One who would teach or preach the sweet Gospel of Jesus Christ effectively must first have tasted the sweetness of that Gospel of the forgiveness of sins in their own life. You must first stand as a repentant, forgiven sinner before you can effectively call others to repentance and announce forgiveness in the name of Jesus Christ. Moreover, as a member of the team of church workers you also serve under the rules and policies of this congregation, its school, and the District of which it is a member. Indeed the called servants of the congregation should be examples to the whole flock in upholding and supporting the constitution of the congregation, District, and Synod of which they are members.

V. Share in the Blessings of the Word You Teach

St. Paul's second illustration is that of a farmer. He writes, "The hard-working farmer . . . ought to have the first share of the crops" (2 Tim. 2:6 RSV). The blessings of God that your ministry brings to your students and to all those whom you serve are also blessings in which you yourself share. The peace of God, which you want to bring to others, should also come to you. The joy of salvation, which you want others to experience, you should also be experiencing. The blessed hope of eternal life, which you want others to gain from the teaching of the Word, must also, by the grace of God, first come to you. And the certainty of the forgiveness of sins, which you teach others through the Gospel of Jesus Christ, must also be partaken of by you. That is the greatest fringe benefit of all in working with and teaching the Word of God: as you study its promsies and learn more and more of the riches of God's love and wisdom, you are first a partaker before you are a dispenser.

Finally, St Paul writes in verse 7 (RSV): "Think over what I say," that is, "ponder it and the Lord will give you understanding." What a blessed promise! When you think over and meditate on God's Word, the Lord Himself will give you understanding. The same truth is expressed in another way in Ps. 111:10 (KJV): "The fear of the Lord is the beginning of wisdom." Remember how King Solomon prayed that the Lord would give him wisdom and understanding in order to serve, to rule God's people well, and to carry out the assignment that God had given him? The Lord granted his petition and made him the wisest man of all. This same Lord says to you, "Ponder My Word and promises and you will get understanding"—the understanding you need to fulfill your high calling as a Christian teacher of the Word and a servant to God and His people. May you be strengthened by that Word as you follow a personal spiritual training program and as you strive to communicate that Word for the nurture of others. May God richly bless you in your ministry of teaching in this congregation and make you a blessing to your pupils, your fellow teachers, your pastor, and to the whole congregation. Amen.

Michael J. Stelmachowicz

Related Scripture readings

John 21:15-17   1 Cor. 12:27-31   Mark 10:13-16

Suggested hymns

"Let Children Hear the Mighty Deeds"
"Christ Is Made the Sure Foundation"
"God's Word Is Our Great Heritage"
"Thou Art the Way; to Thee Alone"
"Come, Holy Ghost, Creator Blest"

LAY EMPHASIS SUNDAY

There's a Hole in the Roof

LUKE 5:18-26

Today's text describes a miraculous healing that took place early in Christ's ministry in Capernaum, described in Matthew's account as "Jesus' own city." It was after Jesus had been rejected by the people of Nazareth, His native city, and had shifted His home and His operation to Capernaum. Jesus had already performed some miracles and was becoming known as a person who did great things to help people. He had healed Peter's mother-in-law. He had driven evil spirits out of a man who was possessed, and earlier in this chapter we read of Jesus' summoning the twelve to be His followers and also healing a man who was afflicted with leprosy.

I. It's Important for Us to Care About Other People

The healing of the paralytic is described in three of the four gospels:

Matthew, Mark, and Luke. John doesn't mention it. One interesting facet of this healing of the paralytic—not found in Matthew's narrative but mentioned by Mark and Luke—is the thought that I have selected as our emphasis for today. It's the fact that the four friends of this man—Mark tells us there were four—who were carrying their friend's bed to Jesus, couldn't get into the house because of the crowd of people, and so they had to go up and literally let the man down through the roof.

In order to understand this better, we have to know a little about the architecture of houses in that day. One Bible commentator says: "They dragged the sick man to the housetop. The oriental houses were built of stone, with a flat roof, on which the so-called upper room was situated, and a stairway often led up from the outside. If this house had no outside stairway, one near it did. Since the houses adjoined, it was easy to pass from one roof to the next, so the paralytic was carried to a place on the roof, directly above where Jesus was in the room below. There they made a hole in the roof by taking the tiles away, and then they let the man down."

I can almost picture the scene. Imagine standing there, crowded into the house, and Jesus is talking. All of a sudden we notice that part of the roof is being taken away, and when the hole is large enough, here comes a bed that is being let down by four ropes. It comes down right in front of Jesus; and there, lying on the bed, is a paralytic, a man who cannot move, who's completely paralyzed. We could never forget such an event. We'd always remember the hole in the roof. That hole in the roof has a message for us today. It tells us many important things.

First of all, it tells us that we need to care about people. That's a message we need in our day and age. We need to be concerned about people. We read in the Gospel narrative that Jesus saw their faith—the faith of these four men—and acted. This indicates that He approved and was glad to see that they cared about this man and believed that Jesus could help him.

At first glance it may seem unusual that several friends should form a committee to bring a handicapped person to Christ. And yet what is more natural than that those who were closest to the palsied man and cared about him should make it possible for him to get to his divine Healer? They didn't wait for Jesus to search him out personally, but they were the hands and feet of the Lord in reaching the man in need.

The church's ministry is not to be performed only by the ordained ministers, but fellow members of the body of Christ serve Christ by serving one another, and as they help anyone in need they are doing it for Christ. Here are laymen at work performing a vital ministry. Where would the palsied man have been without such friends? And where would those who are sick, lonely, depressed, and elderly among our acquaintances be without us?

Before Jesus died on the cross in payment for our sins, He said to His followers: "This is My commandment, that you love one another as I have loved you" (John 15:12 RSV). The love of Jesus was more than words. He didn't simply stand there and sing, "Blest be the tie that binds our hearts in Christian love," He did somthing to show that He loved us. He went out of His way to give His life for you and me. And now He expects us to go out of our way for each other. As we learn to appreciate God's love for us, and all that our heavenly Father has done to rescue us and make us His people, we will love each other as Christ has loved us.

When I talk about this, I have to think about the story of the two bears. A man and his wife were continually quarreling and squabbling. It was a common thing for the neighbors to call the police because of the disturbance in their house—and then all of a sudden things changed. Nobody heard them fighting and quarreling anymore. When a friend asked the wife about it she answered with a chuckle: "Well, everything has changed since two bears came to live with us." The friend said: "What do you mean, two bears?" She answered, "Well, actually, it's two Bible passages—'Bear ye one another's burdens' and 'Forbearing one another in love.' " Yes, two bears! If only those two bears would live in our homes oftener we might learn to overlook each other's faults and love one another as Christ loved us. We would show the same kind of concern for each other that the four men showed for their paralytic friend. That's one message of the hole in the roof.

II. People Are More Important than Buildings

The second thing that the hole in the roof tells us is that people are more important than things. You may think that's a trite thing to say. After all, who doesn't know that? But do we show it? Let's take another look at what's happening! All of a sudden somebody says: "Look what they're doing to that roof. That's vandalism!" Forgetting entirely that the roof is not nearly as important as the person who is being lowered down to Jesus.

Don't each of us, in one way or another, often do the very same thing? We so often get our priorities all mixed up, paying more attention to things instead of people. What about the father who is so busy making a living that he doesn't have time to do things with his children? Or the mother who is so concerned about having the house spic-and-span that the children become neurotics, afraid to touch anything because everything has to be in its place? I could go on and on. We have to admit that all too often things are more important than people. The hole in the roof wants to teach us that people are much more important than things.

III. We Can Expect Results When We Go to God

Third, the hole in the roof reminds us that when we come to God for help, we are not disappointed. He knows our needs, and He takes care of them. Sometime ago I saw a road sign that simply read: "It doesn't cost, it pays." Of course, that's an advertising gimmick, but it's true of our lives as children of God, too. It doesn't cost us to be God's people; it pays to be the children of God. Let's start talking about how wonderful it is to be children of God instead of always talking about all that is involved in being a Christian. Let's tell people what a privilege it is to be the people of God and to enjoy His blessings continually.

It paid the paralytic man to be brought to Jesus. He didn't leave that building the way he entered it. He was let down through the hole in the roof, but he walked out the front door carrying his bed. He walked out and praised God. The text says: The man "departed to his own house, glorifying God" (Luke 5:25 KJV).

Earlier in this chapter we read about Jesus healing a leper. It says that Jesus charged him to tell no man. The next part of that narrative goes on: "but so much the more went there a fame abroad of Him: and great multitudes came together to hear, and to be healed by Him of their infirmities." Jesus knew people well. If you want them not to tell, they tell. So often the same is true of us: the things that are easiest to tell are the things we've been told not to tell. Whether this is what Jesus had in mind really doesn't matter. The important thing is that the paralytic told people what God had done for him. That hole in the roof reminds us that we have a job to do; that we need to tell people about the wonderful things that God has done for us.

IV. Forgiveness Is the Greatest Blessing of All

Not only does the hole in the roof tell us that we should be concerned about other people, that people are more imoprtant than things, and that God will hear and answer our prayers, but it also tells us that we have a God who forgives. And that's more important than anything else.

The man on the bed was lowered down to Jesus. The room was quiet, and Jesus spoke. What did He say? Did He say: "Young man, I say unto you, arise!"? No, He looks at the man and says: "Son, be of good cheer, your sins are forgiven!" (cf. Matt. 9:5). Your sins are forgiven! That's what that man needed more than healing of the body, and you and I need forgiveness more than anything else. We know and feel it inside of ourselves. In spite of our best efforts, we can't live holy and perfect lives. We are, as we confess in our liturgy, poor, miserable sinners who deserve God's punishment. The hole in the roof reminds us that we have a God who forgives, who loves us and removes our sins. Some people say the Gospel is simply good news for a bad situation but we know that isn't true. The Gospel is precious. It's the most important part of our Christian religion. We have a God who loves us and forgives our sins. It is for us to accept His love and forgiveness. The life of that paralytic was never the same again, because he accepted God's forgiveness. He had it all. He had forgiveness of his sins, and he had a sound body, but forgiveness was the most important. When we wonder if God forgives our sins, when we wonder if God still loves us, we need only to look at that hole in the roof and be assured that God for Jesus' sake forgives—and forgives—and forgives—and forgives. Amen.

Willard A. Roth, layman
St. Luke Lutheran Church
St. Louis, Mo.

Related Scripture readings

Matt. 18:5, 18-20   John 13:1—17:20   Phil. 1:3-11   Eph. 4:25—5:2

Suggested hymns

"Blest Be the Tie That Binds"
"What a Friend We Have in Jesus"
"Take My Life and Let It Be"
"My Faith Looks Up to Thee"
"Dear Lord, to Thy True Servants Give"
"From All That Dwell Below the Skies"

ORDINATION AND INSTALLATION OF A PASTOR

Vision for Mission

IS. 6:1-8

Today you, [name of pastor], begin your mission as a called minister of Jesus Christ, for today you enter the office of the holy ministry by ordination on the basis of a call from this congregation, and you are being installed as the pastor of this congregation. You are to preach and teach the Word of God, baptize, and distribute Holy Communion. You are to warn the members of this congregation publicly and privately of how sin endangers their lives, you are to comfort them with the good news of God's love for them in Jesus Christ, and you are to guide them in the way they are to live. This is your mission.

Today you, the members of this congregation, begin your mission under the leadership of this pastor. You are to listen attentively to the Word of God he brings you and to make use of the sacraments he administers among you. You are to take seriously the warnings about sin that he utters, you are to believe the Gospel of God's love that he proclaims, and you are to honor God and support His church by living a Christian life. This is your mission.

So the mission facing all of you, pastor-elect and people, is a challenging one. But it is no more challenging than the mission the prophet Isaiah faced. Seven-hundred fifty years before the birth of Christ, Isaiah was told to go to the people of Judah and to speak God's punishment to them. The people of Judah had made an alliance with Egypt in an effort to ward off the attacks of the Assyrians, who were making a shambles of the world. But God's judgment was coming upon Judah because they had put their trust not in God but in human alliances. Yet Isaiah was also to announce God's mercy to every repentant subject of the kingdom of Judah. But the people of Judah paid no attention to what Isaiah said. In the verses following our text Isaiah is told to say to them that they are hearing but do not understand, and they are seeing but do not perceive. Isaiah's mission was a challenging one.

How was he able to carry it out? God enabled him. God let Isaiah see a wonderful vision. That vision made his mission possible.

If you, pastor-elect and people, are to carry out your mission, you will need a vision. God has not promised to let you see in every detail what Isaiah saw—a throne, smoke, angels, tongs, and burning coals. But in our text God gives you a vision of Himself. That is the vision Isaiah needed, and that is the vision you need. For it is a vision of God as holy, gracious, and powerful. Here is a

Vision for Mission

Here is the vision that makes your mission possible.

I.

The vision for mission is a vision of God as holy. Isaiah saw the Lord, high and lifted up, sitting on a throne, more resplendent than the throne of any earthly king. His train, His flowing robe, filled the temple. Around Him were angels, strange creatures called seraphim, which had six wings. With two they covered their face, as if to hide their eyes from the radiancy of God's glory. With two they covered their feet, as if to show that God's ways are ultimately mysterious. And with two they flew, as if to indicate that they were not above God but under God, serving Him. And all the while they cried out to each other, "Holy, holy, holy is the Lord of hosts," with such force that the foundations of the building shook and the house filled with smoke. An awesome sight! A vision of God as the holy One.

We often speak about a loving God. Sometimes we forget that He is a holy God too. He is without sin, absolutely just, and very demanding. He demands that His law, the Ten Commandments, be kept perfectly, not only in words and deeds but in thoughts. If a person were able to keep all the commandments and then broke only one, he would be guilty of all. Anyone who transgresses any of God's commandments in any way, or fails to do what they demand, sins and suffers the consequences.

Where does that leave us? Isaiah knew where it left him. He cried out: "Woe is me! For I am lost," I am cut off, destroyed, "for I am a man of unclean lips and I dwell in the midst of a people of unclean lips" (Is. 6:5 RSV). I cannot bear to be in the presence of the holy God. How then can I carry out His mission? Divine eloquence issuing from my lips? Impossible! Isaiah was keenly aware of his sinfulness.

So are we when we look at ourselves in the mirror of God's law. We have fallen short of God's standard. We have not measured up. We are not perfect. We, too, are people of unclean lips. Our lips are no better than our heart, which, the Bible says, is desperately wicked.

That's why our words have not always been truthful. In our rush to keep the peace and in our desire to prevent the rocking of the boat of human relationships we've resorted to little white lies. We've engaged in distortion and overstatement to get someone to believe something that isn't true. If a pest calls you on the phone and you don't want to talk to him and you tell your wife to tell him you're not at home, that's a lie. If you mess up a job and you explain it to your boss by saying it was the fault of the sales department or the working conditions or something, that's a lie. We may have gotten into the habit of lying so often that we think nothing of it.

And we teach others to lie. A woman who had trouble with her daughter said, "I don't know where that child ever learned to lie." But the child had heard her mother say, "There's that horrible Mrs. Doakes coming; I wish that woman would keep her face out of this house." The mother cleared up as rapidly as she could—straightening up, putting things in closets, tidying the house. When the bell rang, the mother opened the door and cried out, "Oh, Mrs. Doakes, it's so good to see you. It's nice of you to drop in!" Where did her daughter learn to lie?

Even a gray lie or a white lie is not justified in God's sight. We are sinful people because we have not always been scrupulously honest in our speech. Woe to us! We cannot stand before the holy God. "Holy, holy, holy is the Lord of hosts!" (Is. 6:3 RSV).

But if the vision of God as holy only makes us aware of our sinfulness, how can it be a vision for mission? How can it help you carry out your mission? In this way: when you see God as holy, you see your need of God's help. The people who know they need God's help are the people God helps and makes effective in His mission. Recall some of the people who have been effective in God's mission. Moses said that he was slow of speech and tongue and therefore unable to be God's spokesman to the children of Israel. Jeremiah complained that he was only a child and therefore unable to do what God would have him do. Peter cried out, after seeing the miraculous catch of fish, "Depart from me, for I am a sinful man, O Lord!" (Luke 5:8 RSV). None of these men said, "I can do so much that God can hardly do without me. I can do so much good that God will have to reward me." No. They knew what they were before God. You, pastor-elect and people, will not be effective in God's mission if you say, "We are so virtuous, so talented, so capable that God must be glad we're lined up with Him." The people God uses best in His mission are those who know that they don't deserve even to be in God's mission. The vision of God as holy helps you carry out your mission because it leads you to see your need of God's help.

That need is urgent. If God hadn't come to Isaiah's rescue, the mission would have been impossible for him. Sin can so intimidate and degrade us as to make us incapable of any service to God or people. That's why God saw to it that the vision was not only of Himself as holy but also as gracious. God, the gracious one—here is a vision for mission.

II.

To say that God is gracious means that God forgives. That's what God did for Isaiah. Listen to what Isaiah says: "Then flew one of the seraphim to me, having in his hand a burning coal which he had taken with tongs from the altar. And he touched my mouth, and said: 'Behold, this has touched your lips; your guilt is taken away, and your sin forgiven' " (Is. 6:6-7 RSV)

Sin can be forgiven. No man can do it. No angel can. But God can. The angel, as God's servant, took a burning coal from the altar. The burning coal symbolized the cleansing fire of God's love. A touch of that love was sufficient. The burning coal merely touched Isaiah's mouth, but with that touch came God's own sure word of forgiveness. God had accepted Isaiah despite his imperfection, inconsistency, and inadequacy. Isaiah was God's own man. How did this vision of God as gracious affect Isaiah? When God called out, "Whom shall I send, and who will go for us?" Isaiah quickly responded, "Here am I! Send me" (Is. 6:8 RSV). He was ready to carry out the mission.

You, pastor-elect and people, are ready to carry out your mission because you have seen the vision of God as gracious. You have seen it in Holy Scripture. Before your eyes has stood a cross, on a hill outside the city of Jerusalem, a cross on which God offered His dearest and His best. In the death of Jesus Christ God demonstrated His love for the whole human race. We have only to be touched by that love to be cleansed from all our sin. You were touched by that love in Holy Baptism. As you've grown older, you've had many more contacts with it—each time you saw a child baptized, each time you heard the Gospel, each time you received Holy Communion. Along with that touch has come God's own word of forgiveness to you, "Your guilt is taken away, and your sin forgiven."

"Man, that's a heavy sound," sighed a bearded youth who had tried dropping out via drugs.

"I've tried doing everything," confided a young married woman. "but no matter how much good I do, I still haven't paid for what I did to my folks. I still see the hurt in their eyes and I feel guilty all over again."

The beauty of God's forgiveness is that He not only takes sin away but every ounce of guilt as well. It's a daily forgiveness. There's no need to pile up evils over a long period to set before Him. You can give Him each offense each day and know that you're forgiven. You're forgiven even though you blow it endless times by failing to live up to your ethical standard. God doesn't want long brooding over your sins or unhealthy preoccupation with them. He wants you to confess them and to sense His gracious forgiveness. God wants you to be certain that He has accepted you in spite of what you are and what you have done.

How does this vision of God as gracious make your mission possible? It frees you from guilt. You don't have to live with an accusing conscience. You don't have to constantly prove your own goodness or defend your own worth before God or anyone else. You don't have to earn any favors from God. You already have His favor. You are forgiven. You may not always feel forgiven, but God's love doesn't change. His grace is the same every day. Remember what Jesus said, "He who has seen Me has seen the Father" (John 14:9 RSV). Through Jesus Christ God continues to reveal Himself to you as a loving Father, a forgiving God. You are God's own man, woman, or child. That vision makes your mission possible.

It doesn't make your mission easy. Certainly, Isaiah's mission was not easy. The people to whom he went were obstinate, he was subjected to a lot of inconvenience and finally a martyr's death. There must have been times when Isaiah felt his own weakness and doubted his power to carry out the mission. That's why it was so important for him to see the vision of God also as powerful.

III.

Isaiah saw the vision of God as powerful when the seraphim circled the throne crying: "The whole earth is full of His glory" (Is. 6:3 RSV). Glory here is another word for power. The whole earth is full of God's power. The power of God is seen in nature—in floods, droughts, earthquakes, and tornadoes. The power of God is seen in the lives of individual people, when He protects them from harm and delivers them from danger. The power of God is seen in God's mission, in the Christian church. When God brings His Word and Sacraments to people, God brings almighty power. Through the Word and the Sacraments God works to perform wonders, to bring people from unbelief to faith, from a life of sin to a life of holiness. The whole earth, nature and human life and the Christian church, is full of God's power. That vision helped Isaiah carry out his mission.

You too, pastor-elect and people, need the vision of God's power, for there will come days when you sense your weakness and doubt your power to carry out the mission. There will be times when you, the pastor, will say, "My love is so cold, my prayers are so sluggish. I wish I could be more faithful in my work. I wish I could share Jesus Christ more effectively. I wish I could be a better pastor. I wonder if I have what it takes to be in God's mission." There will be days when you, individual members of this congregation, will say, "It's so hard to live as a Christian these days. I wish I would take God's Word more seriously. I wish I could be more faithful to God and His church. There's so much indifference to spiritual things in my own life. And certainly, many outside the church seem completely indifferent to Christ and His Word. I wonder if I have what it takes to be in God's mission."

Two friends were trying to find out why their car wouldn't run. They tore the whole engine down. Finally one exclaimed, "Hey, Bill! I found the problem. We're out of gas." Our main problem today is not war, race, genetics, pollution, or outer space. It's a spiritual problem. We've run out of God. We've run out of gas.

There are all sorts of power. Without gas, our cars are not empowered to run. Without Lake Mead, Hoover Dam could not provide electrical power through its turbines for Arizona, Nevada, and California. Without the pellets of fissionable material that make up the bundles used in atomic plants there would not be power to make power. So too, we in God's mission are powerless without God's power.

But God's power is available. And it is abundant. When I was a boy growing up in Ashtabula, Ohio, on the main line of the New York Central, I enjoyed watching the long freight trains come through. I knew the schedules of the trains and would often ride my bicycle to the station to watch the huge engines come pounding down the track with their hundred or more cars behind. The strength and power harnessed to those steam engines was something I'll never forget.

Yet in our text we have a vision of even greater power. And God is still the same powerful God He was in Isaiah's day. He is still our refuge and our strength, a very present help in trouble.

During the voyage of an American liner across the Atlantic a storm arose, and in the terrific gale a sailor was washed overboard. Instantly the cry went up, "Man overboard!" One of the crew with presence of mind seized a rope having a loop at the end, and threw it over the stern. The captain shouted, "Have you got the rope?" And the reply came, "No, the rope has got me." The drowning sailor, when he caught the rope, had passed the loop over his shoulders and under his arms, being too weak to hold it, and the loop kept him from sinking.

No matter how weak we are, God won't let us sink. He says to us:

> Fear not, I am with thee, oh, be not dismayed;
> For I am thy God and will still give thee aid;
> I'll strengthen thee, help thee, and cause thee to stand,
> Upheld by My righteous, omnipotent hand.
>
> When through the deep waters I call thee to go,
> The rivers of sorrow shall not overflow;
> For I will be with thee thy troubles to bless
> And sanctify to thee thy deepest distress.
>
> When through fiery trials thy pathway shall lie,
> My grace, all-sufficient, shall be thy supply.
> The flames shall not hurt thee; I only design
> Thy dross to consume and thy gold to refine. *(TLH* 427:3-5)

That is the kind of God we have. He uses even the difficulties in the mission to strengthen our faith. He will never leave us. Underneath, always, are the everlasting arms.

And so, pastor-elect and people, you are ready to carry out your mission, for you have seen the vision. It is a vision of God as holy, God as gracious, God as powerful. That vision makes your mission possible. Amen.   Gerhard Aho

Related Scripture readings

Luke 5:1-11   Eph. 4:7-16   2 Cor. 4:1-6   2 Cor. 5:16-21

Suggested hymns

"Lord of the Church, We Humbly Pray"
"Isaiah, Mighty Seer, in Days of Old"
"God of the Prophets, Bless the Prophets' Sons"
"One Thy Light, the Temple Filling"

STEWARDSHIP

Great Is Thy Faithfulness

LAM. 3:22-24

One of the truly great Christian classics is John Bunyan's novel, *The Pilgrim's Progress.* In the story, Bunyan reports how in a dream he saw a man named Christian meet a man named Faithful. Christian and Faithful journeyed for some time as good companions until they reached the city Vanity Fair. At Vanity Fair, all sorts of delights were for sale, for example, houses, lands, trades, honors, preferments, titles, countries, lusts, pleasures, delights, gold, silver, precious gems, and souls. Soon the two of them were in trouble in the town because of their Christian testimony. A trial was ordered. The jury consisted of Mr. No-good, Mr. Blind-man, Mr. Love-lust, Mr. Malice, Mr. Liar, Mr. Enmity, Mr. Cruelty, and Mr. Live-loose, Mr. Heady, Mr. High-mind, Mr. Hate-light, and Mr. Implacable. Faithful was found guilty and was condemned to death by torture. Bunyan reports what happened next: "Now I saw that there stood behind the multitude a chariot and a couple of horses waiting for Faithful, who (so soon as his adversaries had despatched him) was taken up into it, and straightway was carried up through the clouds, with sound of trumpets, the nearest way to the Celestial Gate." Faithful had lived up to his name. He had in a small way mirrored the faithfulness of his God. Great is God's faithfulness! We are thrilled here at our congregation to find stewards of God whom we may call "faithful"!

When Jeremiah wrote our text, he had plenty of reasons to question the faithfulness of God. He had ample cause to wonder what had happened to the promises of God since Jerusalem had fallen to the Babylonians. Multitudes of the people had been deported to another country. Those left behind were starving to death. The situation was almost unbelievable, with mothers eating their own children. Priests were slain before the altar in God's temple. Aliens had overrun the Holy City and the sacred had been profaned. Jeremiah might have blamed God for allowing this to happen. Yet he had to confess that they had brought it all on themselves. He wrote, "Jerusalem sinned grievously, therefore she became filthy; all who honored her despise her, for they have seen her nakedness; yea, she herself groans, and turns her face away" (Lam. 1:8 RSV). Like the proverbial chickens, their sins had come home to roost, and the hour of God's judgment had come.

Our nation does not yet have all the problems that the Jews had. We do have some that linger on, however. We have problems that continue to eat away, like a cancer, or like rats gnawing away at foundation timbers. From here and there we are told: "Get ready for a lower standard of living." President Carter warned against a national crisis of confidence. Many people do not believe that America can deal effectively with its problems. The issue is such that he wanted to encourage us to "say something good about your country."

Other issues also trouble the Christian heart. Divorces almost equal the number of marriages. There are more and more single-parent homes with the extra burden of responsibilities that attend them. Many are choosing "alternative life-styles." Sliding moral values must grieve the Christian who sees God has sanctioned only two life-styles: single and married! If you believe that these are only national problems that do not apply to you, then I suggest that you read your newspaper more carefully and listen to the local news! We are ready to confess, "Great is Thy faithfulness [Lam. 3:23 RSV], O Lord, but could we have some help?"

With all of these fctors comng to bear upon our lives, how can God expect us to be faithful in our stewardship? Jeremiah, have you a good word for us? His response comes back from the text, "Yes!" Jeremiah rises to the occasion and from his own painful vantage point says, "The steadfast love of the Lord never ceases" (Lam. 3:22 RSV). One of the most difficult truths to appropriate for yourself is that God loves you. He loves you not because I say it, but because He says it. God loves you. It is hard to believe because we do not feel worthy of His love. God's love for us does not depend on our worthiness. If it did, God would love none of us. St. Paul echoes Jeremiah's thought: "Who shall separate us from the love of Christ? Shall tribulation, or distress, or persecution, or famine, or nakedness, or peril, or sword? ... No, in all these things we are more than conquerors through Him who loved us. . . . [Nothing] will be able to separate us from the love of God in Christ Jesus our Lord" (Rom. 8:35-39 RSV).

The ultimate proof of God's faithful love for us is shown in His sending Jesus Christ. Jesus, by his cross, death, and resurrection, proved God's faithfulness and dealt with our unfaithfulness. In Jesus, the sinner finds everything needed:

> —His faithfulness for my unfaithfulness;
> —His forgiveness for my guilt;
> —His cleansing for my impurity;
> —His power for my weakness;
> —His courage for my fear;
> —His love for my bitterness;
> —His victory for my defeat.

In Christ, all of the promises of God find their faithful and resounding, "Yes!" Put your trust in Him!

Jeremiah goes on to tell of the faithfulness of God, saying "His mercies never come to an end; they are new every morning" (Lam. 3:22-23 RSV). What mercies of the Lord did you rise to enjoy this morning? Did you rise to find strength of body and soul adequate for the day? Did you rise to enjoy the sunshine? How about the fresh air? Did you rise to find a refrigerator and pantry stocked with good things for your enjoyment? Did you observe on your way to church this morning the trees and God's daily art show? Thank Him whose mercies are new every day!

Because God's mercies are faithfully granted, you can be faithful in using them. God gives you your time. He gives you your talents. Now is the time to recommit them to His service. Will you willingly share your abilities for the good of your brothers and sisters, and the benefit of Christ's kingdom?

A young ministerial student was spending his summer working for the National Park Service. Among his duties was that of conducting Sunday morning worship. The congregation was composed of vacationers and campers. One Sunday, because there was no regular pianist, he asked for a volunteer. No one responded. He then asked, "Is there anyone here who would like to volunteer the musical ability of someone else?" A teenaged girl replied, "My dad can play the piano." After hesitating a moment, a tall distinguished gentleman walked down the aisle. As he began to accompany the singing it became apparent that he was playing the piano with only one finger. He never missed a note and his timing was perfect. At the end of the service, the assembly learned that their pianist was a noted surgeon from a distant city. It struck them all that this skilled doctor had offered to them without shame or apology the one God-given musical talent that he possessed—making no excuse that he didn't have more to offer, he had given in full measure what God had given to him. This is all that God expects! Faithful stewardship of time and talents at our congregation this year may get us some "one finger piano players," but we'll have plenty of kingdom workers and they'll be using their talents and not hiding behind the tired old excuse, "Someone else can do it better than I can."

God's mercies are fresh every morning. On the basis of His years of faithfulness to you, you can believe in a continuation of His mercies—if not quantitatively, then in the quality of His presence. Think back over the years of your life and the faithfulness of your God. Recall how He has stood by you through thick and thin. In reflecting, your heart can be braced against some of the insecurities that parade across the daily headlines. They won't shock you into paralysis. Our God is faithful. We have observed that. Nothing can get to you that hasn't first gotten past Him. One Christian said, "The years teach a wisdom that the days never know." You can mark God's faithfulness when you celebrate another birthday or another wedding anniversary.

Lastly, Jeremiah looks up from Jerusalem's rubble, reflects on the faithfulness of God, and says, "I will hope in Him" (Lam. 3:24 RSV). A sign of hope from God is desperately needed in our times when there are so many signs of confusion and futility. Contemporary novels and dramas are often characterized by the word "absurd." Life is portrayed as hopeless. Adequate answers cannot be found for man's pressing dilemmas. Suicide is thought to be the way of courage. Holy Scripture knows nothing of that sort of hopelessness. It knows that life without Christ is a hopeless end. Life with Christ is an endless hope. It recognizes with the psalmist, "I had fainted unless I had beleved to see the goodness of the Lord in the land of the living" (Ps. 27:13 KJV). With God's hope demonstrated at the cross of Christ and His empty tomb, we are assured that God's side is eventually going to win. It is going to win because God's faithfulness is great. As God is faithful to us, He enables us by His good Spirit to be and to remain faithful stewards of all of His gifts for all of our days.

Near the end of the Second Part of *The Pilgrim's Progress* Bunyan describes the death of another Christian, Mr. Valiant-for-truth, as follows: "Mr. Valiant-for-truth . . . said: ' . . . My sword I give to him that shall succeed me in my pilgrimage, and my courage and skill to him that can get it. My marks and scars I carry with me to be a witness for me that I have fought His battles who now will be my Rewarder.' When the day that he must go hence was come, many accompanied him to the riverside; into which as he went, he said, 'Death, where is thy sting?' And as he went down deeper, he said, 'Grave, where is thy victory?' So he passed over, and all the trumpets sounded for him on the other side." Great is God's faithfulness! Amen.   James T. Hoppes

Related Scripture readings

Ps. 136   Lam. 3:19-24   Luke 12:22-34   Rom. 8:31-29

Suggested hymns

"O God, Thou Faithful God"
"Praise, Oh, Praise Our God and King"
"O Lord of Heaven and Earth and Sea"
"Take My Life and Let It Be"
"Abide, O Dearest Jesus"

WEDDING

Leaving and Cleaving

GEN. 2:24

When it comes to the subject of marriage, there seems to be no end of words! Thousands of books have been written on the subject, and still they continue to come off the press. One hears and reads so much on the subject that it eventually becomes confusing. What one so-called authority proposes, another disposes, until we begin to long for a few, clear, authoritative words of direction.

We have such clear and authoritative words in the text. They are clear in that the directives are sharp and to the point. They are authoritative because they come from the Author of marriage, God Himself. And they are few in number. In fact, they can be summarized in two words: "leave" and "cleave"! "A man leaves his father and his mother and cleaves to his wife, and they become one flesh" (Gen. 2:24 RSV). That's it! That's God's own directive for marriage. And so, on this happy occasion in your life, we want to think about the implications of these directives as we consider the theme: "Leaving and Cleaving!"

The dictionary offers several definitions for these words, some of which are applicable to your marriage and others of which are not. For example, the word "leave" carries the definitions "to go away from, to abandon." The first of these definitions—to go away from—is certainly applicable to marriage. The husband "goes away from" *his* family of origin and the wife "goes away from" *her* family of origin. Most books on marriage suggest that this "going away from" be done in geographic terms, that the bride and groom put some mileage between themselves and their families of origin. This is in no way a judgment upon the families of origin. It is rather a recognition of the fact that if you are to learn to become dependent on each other, you will need to break your dependencies on your respective homes. Many difficulties arise in marriage when one or the other—or sometimes *both* spouses—have failed to "leave" father and mother.

But this "leaving" is not just geographical. It is also, and perhaps more importantly, psychological. The basic realationship in God's plan is that of husband and wife. The parent-child relationship is a very different kind of relationship, a very necessary and important temporary arrangement, but only a temporary one. Ultimately, it must be replaced or at least made secondary to the *new* relationship of husband and wife. If you accept this God-given arrangement, you will be saved from trying to organize your lives around two centers, from being torn between two loyalties. There never need be any question about whose wishes should be considered or where your duty lies. The new love and the new home always take priority.

But while "leaving" father and mother means "to go away from"—psychologically, if not geographically—it does *not* mean "to abandon" them. Our parents are still parents after marriage and they will remain so throughout our lives. None of us grows up in a vacuum. We have our families, and our families are important to us. A husband needs to remember that his wife's family is important to her; and a wife needs to remember that her husband's family is important to him. So you will not expect each other to abandon these relationships. Instead you will love and respect your spouse's parents as people who are important in your spouse's life. So "leaving" means "to go away from," not "to abandon"!

Wise parents *let* their children leave, let their children "go away from" them. Tough as it may be, parents who truly love their children will take themselves sternly in hand and master the impulse to cling to them. The weeks may see long for a while without visits, or at least phone calls, but wise parents will not demand them. Sometimes parents whose children have married are sure that their son is not being properly fed, that their daughter has to work too hard, that the money is unwisely spent, that health is endangered, and so on and on. But they must not say so! They must let their children *leave* them—go away from them—in order that the children can establish a healthy dependence on each other in their marriage. There's an old adage that says, "Live and let live!" When it comes to the responsibilities of children and parents at the time of marriage, the adage could be altered slightly to read: "Leave and *let* leave!"

But "leaving" is only the first part of God's directive in our text. The second part is "cleaving." Here again the dictionary offers definitions that are both applicable and inapplicable to marriage. One dictionary offers these definitions for cleave: "to adhere to, to cling to, to be faithful to." Cleaving in the sense of "adhering to" is certainly appropriate in marriage. In fact, our text speaks of this adhering in terms of "becoming one flesh." "A man leaves his father and his mother and cleaves to his wife, and they become one flesh." Something profound happens to two persons who enter into marriage. Their change in status is so basic that it is no longer accurate or proper to speak of them as two. "They are no longer two but one," says Jesus (Mark 10:8 RSV).

This "oneness" will need to be nourished throughout your married life together. Many forces are at work in society today that tend to pull married people apart. Some forces also within the marriage relationship put a strain on the "oneness" prescribed in Scripture. Since you come from different backgrounds and have different desires and needs, tensions along the way are inevitable. When these tensions arise, you need to realistically face what you are and who you are. You are sinful human beings who would like to see the world—and your spouse—revolve completely around you and your desires and needs. When both parties in the marriage operate with this desire, you end up with two egocentric and separate circles that don't include the other. The only way those circles of self-concern can be broken is by repentance and the entrance of God's grace and forgiveness, which enables us to break out of our own little circle to embrace the other, and to reestablish the "oneness" for which God created us in marriage. So "cleaving" in the sense of "adhering to" is important for your marriage.

The second definition for "cleave"—to cling to—would need some qualification. The word "cling" brings to mind the idea of the "clinging vine," a term defined in Webster as "a woman inclined to be helpless and dependent in her relationship with a man." This kind of *over*dependence can lead to problems in marriage. Both parties in the marriage need to maintain their own individuality while working toward the "oneness" that we spoke of a moment ago. Individuality is an important ingredient in the marriage relationship. It is threatened when the husband looks upon the wife as an extension of himself, or feels that she should find contentment and fulfillment simply in her role as his wife. Individuality is also threatened when the wife—like a clinging vine—tries to live her life through her husband. And so cleaving, in the sense of "clinging to," needs to be handled with care in marriage.

Someone has spoken of the need for both dependence and independence in the marriage relationship. These needs represent two sides of the self. The impulse of the one side of us is to merge—the "urge to merge" as it has been called. That side is called our Merger Self. The opposing impulse is to seek our individuality. That side is called our Seeker Self. It is only by getting these two sides to work in harmony that one becomes capable of both individuality and mutuality in marriage.

Like so many other things in husband-wife relationships, there is a fine line here. Because each marriage represents the bringing together of two unique persons, no one can tell exactly where the "dependence-independence" line is best marked off in any given marriage. It takes careful testing and stretching for each couple to find that line in their own marriage, and you will need to give this your careful attention in the weeks and months that lie ahead.

When we turn from the marriage relationship to our relationship to God, we discover a similar tension between independence and dependence. It was the human drive for independence—independence from God—that initially brought woe upon the human race. Like our first parents, Adam and Eve, we too want to be like God. We want to be the masters of our own fate, the captains of our own souls. At the same time we recognize that we are dependent on God for all that we are and all that we hope to be. So there is a tension in our relationship to God, similar to the tension in marriage between independence and dependence.

When we turn from cleaving in the sense of "clinging" to cleaving in the sense of "being faithful to," we are once again dealing with a meaning that is appropriate for the marriage relationship. As a matter of fact, cleaving in this sense is indispensable to a good marriage. Faithfulness lies at the heart of a good marriage. When both husband and wife are faithful to the other and have complete trust and confidence in the other, a foundation is built that can withstand some of the worst storms of life. Certainly this meaning of "cleave" was included when God gave the command: "A man shall leave his father and mother and be joined to his wife" (Matt. 19:5; Mark 10:7 RSV).

But basic to all your "leaving and cleaving" will be your cleaving to

Christ—adhering to Him and being faithful to Him. Jesus Christ is the Vine to which we, the branches, must cling in faith. But even more importantly, Jesus Himself is the Clinging Vine—in the very best sense of that term—who holds on to us even when we are tempted to let go of Him. That is His promise to us, a promise He gave us in our baptism and a promise that He continually renews for us through Word and Sacrament. "I am the Vine, you are the branches. He who abides in Me, and I in him, he it is that bears much fruit, for apart from Me you can do nothing. . . . As the Father has loved Me, so have I loved you; abide in My love. . . . These things I have spoken to you, that My joy may be in you, and that your joy may be full" (John 15:5, 9, 11 RSV).

When we cling to Christ as He clings to us, the result can only be joy. Small wonder, therefore, that the poet should write:

> O happy home where two, in heart united,
> In holy faith, are clinging unto Thee;
> Where both, to Thee a joyful service bringing,
> Hear and obey Thy voice most willingly;
> Where both, to Thee in truth forever cleaving,
> In joy, in grief, make Thee their only Stay.
> And fondly hope in Thee to be believing
> Both in the good and in the evil day. *(TLH* 626:2)

That is my wish for you as you begin your married life together, as I am sure it is the wish of all your relatives and friends gathered here today! Amen.   Kenneth L. Frerking

Related Scripture readings

Matt. 19:4-6   Mark 10:6-9   John 15:5-11   Eph. 5:31-33

Suggested hymns

"The Voice That Breathed O'er Eden"
"O Father, All Creating"
"O Perfect Love"
"Lord, Who at Cana's Wedding-Feast"
"We Lift Our Hearts, O Father"

FATHER'S DAY

Happy Forgiveness Day

ROM. 6:3-11

Congratulations and best wishes today to those who have attained the lofty and respected state of fatherhood.

As those of us who are fathers accept the adulation, we recognize that we did little to arrive at the fatherly state. Oh, we participated in a biological process alright. We were part of a God-formed creation of a human life. We waited, somewhat anxiously, through the nine months of pregnancy and fidgeted through a delivery. But that was about it. We received no specific training in fathering, took no schooling related to the task, and undertook no activity in preparation for the event. Just, there— one day, as a kind of happenstance of our place as husband, we were fathers.

But that is not to say that being a father is not a noble calling. Far from it; it is noble indeed. Vital, one might say. God-like, in a way. For when Jesus set about to describe God's relationship to us He did not use the word *nursemaid* (which surely would be comfortable for those of us who have trouble growing up), nor *servant* (for those of us who bungle through life waiting to be waited on), nor even *mother* (which would be a great comfort to those of us who would like to snuggle down into the lap of life and avoid any hurt). He calls Him *Father*. And the whole image of the Biblical father as leader and guide, as helper and friend, as giver and sustainer comes to mind.

So we who have becomes fathers certainly have attained a noble state. In fact, we are told that much of what our children become depends on us and our relationship to them. Psychologists claim that much of the inner stability of our children depends on us as fathers and the security we are able to offer them. It is the father, they say, more than the mother, who sets the tone of moral values and attitudes in the home. The father is the significant leader and, some say, the first picture of God that a child forms in his or her mind. In a sense, one could say, that as fathers (and mothers) we are the very reflection of God, as He guides and directs our children through us. We are His agents as we instruct our children, equip them and train them for living and for a life of service. We are the ones who impart to them the Christian values. The Holy Spirit

uses us as instruments in creating in them the faith in Christ that will
sustain them throughout their lives. We are the ones who must strike the
delicate balance between leading and letting go, so that our children will
attain a competent maturity. And—

But wait! Just a minute now! Surely we are not responsible for all of
that. After all, we're only human. Is all of that true? Is all of what our
children become—what they are and how they adjust—is that the direct
result of our working out our roles as parents? Is it true that their ability
to love depends on the efficacy of our love for them, and their ability to
function in the world depends on our adequacy as parents? If that is true;
what can we do to deal with such an impossible situation?

Too often we do the wrong thing. For the most part, we accepted the
statement that we alone are responsible for our children, what they are,
and what they will become. Paralysed by fear, we instruct, correct, and
mold them. Using every power of personality and persuasion we have, we
try to make our children into what we want them to be (lest, of course,
someone find them deficient, and, in the process, find us deficient as
well). "Sit up straight," we say. "Don't do that!" "Behave yourself!" "Do
the right things!" "Stay out of trouble!" "Help . . . Act . . . Be . . ." And
sometimes our parenting turns into a kind of perpetual harangue that is
supposed to make our children into the models of faith, love, and service
we have projected for them.

But, in the midst of the correcting and the helping, the telling and the
scolding, someone throws in something like Father's Day to mess us up.
Look at what we are to be as father (and mother, for that matter). Look
what is designed by the God-model we see in Scripture. God is loving and
accepting, kind and gentle—leader, helper, friend, and confidant. And
dismally we must admit that before the picture of the perfect Father we
fade into a shadowy reflection of what we had intended.

Where there was to be kindness, there is often blaming and scolding.
Where there was to be acceptance, giving and love, there is often
attacking, accusing, and rejection. Where there was to be patience, there is
impatience. Where there was to be control, there is often anger and a
bitter word.

Why? How could it happen? We mean to be better. In our minds we
have an exact picture of the parent we mean to be. What goes wrong?

We confront the absolute truth that the very power we use to try to
make our children into what we want them to be is utterly ineffective in
making us into the parents we mean to be.

Well, Father's day would be a dismal failure indeed if we who are
fathers are congratulated simply as a matter of form and if we accepted
the adulation, knowing full well that we neither deserve nor desire the
attention and praise. Clearly, on most days, even on our most well-
intentioned days, we simply don't deserve the praise. In truth, at the

magnificent task of being a father (or a mother) we are only marginally successful—blundering often, more serving of self than our children, grasping at straws and hopes and dreams that might make up for the inadequacy in both the quantity and quality of our parenting.

But let's not let it slip by like that. Let's do something with this day besides feel good for a while on the outside and bad for a longer while on the inside. There is more to be had here than that.

Our text for today seems, at first glance, to have little to do with Father's Day. It has no fatherly theme, and it mentions nothing about the glories of fatherhood nor the implications of trying to fulfill that role.

But Paul's words from Romans clearly outline the implications of the death of Christ for us in our daily living and doing. We are told that Christ died for us and because of our participation in His death by Baptism, we have now "died to sin" and are freed from slavery to sin and its destruction. We are already re-created by God into the "newness of life" that Christ has purchased for us. We are able now, by the power of the Spirit, to live as the ones who are becoming constantly more and more alive in Christ, and more and more able to evidence that we are children of the resurrection.

It is that powerful proclamation of the Gospel as an ongoing, re-creating power in us that permits us to look at every event and realize that the occasions on which we come to grips with our inadequacy and inability in the face of God's perfection are not times for despair but times for renewal.

Father's Day might be a good occasion for congratulations and a gift and card exchange. But more, it is a time for the renewal of ourselves and parents and the renewal of the relationships in our homes. It is one more chance to bury the old father (parent) and to rejoice in the revitalization and renewal of the parent we were meant to be. The Gospel is hope—hope in the midst of despair. Surely, we can go on desperately trying to make ourselves into perfect parents and our children into perfect offspring. We can go on pushing ourselves and our children, demanding, scolding, and attacking self and one another in a futile attempt to be what we cannot be.

But we have the privilege, as God's people, to stand fearlessly before him and to admit our failures and our needs. We can be assured by the God who has, as our text says, buried us with Christ; that He has already raised us to newness of life.

This day begins forgiven, as does every day. "We know that our old self was crucified with Him so that . . . we might no longer be enslaved to sin. For He who has died is freed from sin." So we can "consider" ourselves "dead to sins and alive to God in Christ Jesus" (Rom. 6:6-7, 11 RSV).

That is the Father's Day gift we *need*—the only gift that will make it possible for us both to accept the acclaim that this day will bring and to begin again tomorrow to undertake the tremendously challenging and vital task of being a parent to our children.

It is only in the honest reflection on the past that we are able to find the renewal in Christ that we need in order to go on. What would our lives be, if we had to bear every mistake, every angry word, every error in judgment, every cruelty, every stupidity from now into the adulthood of our children? What could possibly happen but that an increasing wall of hurts, disappointments, and fears would continue to build between us, until we would be nothing more than strangers to one another.

Surely, no gift is more treasured in the Christian home than the recreating power of the forgiveness given us in Jesus Christ as we share that treasure with one another.

And it *is* Father's Day. What better occasion could there be than this to sit down with our families and do that necessary thing we ought to do often, but too often let slide, ignore, or forget?

What better time than today to say to that group of loving, caring people around us: "Forgive me—my children and my wife—for I have failed to be what God and I intended me to be. I have hurt too often instead of helped; loved myself instead of treasuring my loved ones; served my own needs instead of yours. I have taken you for granted and even expected your love and care for me. Forgive me. And rejoice with me that I am forgiven by our loving God in Jesus Christ."

It's not a bad little exercise—though it may be difficult at first. And the caring that is renewed by the act—the regeneration that might be begun by such an honest confession and celebration of the forgiveness of God in Christ Jesus might become the foundation for a daily opportunity for forgiveness and renewal in our homes.

So, happy Father's Day! A happy day, indeed. For most of us our place as father is a happy one and we gladly celebrate it. Today we remember the treasures given to us by our children and the opportunities and challenges they bring into our lives. But particularly we parents remember the need we have for renewal as we struggle to be fathers (and mothers) to these children of ours. We celebrate today, not our successes in parenting, but the renewal and forgiveness given to each of us as we attempt to be to our children the channels of the active love of God in their lives. Amen.   Theodore W. Schroeder

Related Scripture readings

Gen. 18:19	Deut. 11:18-21	Luke 11:11-13
Deut. 6:7, 20-24	Prov. 22:6	Eph. 6:4

Suggested hymns
"Oh, Blest the House, Whate'er Befall"
"Renew Me, O Eternal Light"
"Jesus I Will Never Leave"
"Blest Be the Tie That Binds"

FOURTH OF JULY/INDEPENDENCE DAY

God and/or Caesar

MARK 12:17

Taxes are always a bother. Especially annoying is a poll tax. That is the kind referred to in the record of the incident from which today's text is taken. In the days of our Lord it was called a "census" and was levied on every adult to provide funds for Caesar's coffers. It served to remind every Jew that he lived under pagan rule.

Paying this tax obviously created theological problems in Israel. Zealots simply refused to pay it; they would rather fight. Sadducees paid, but reluctantly. Pharisees debated the issue at great length but offered no further resistance. Herodians usually sided with Rome and so submitted to the levy as a political fact of life.

Some Herodians and some Pharisees came to Jesus one day to pose the question of paying the poll tax. They were sure they could put Jesus into a no-win situation. If He answered yes, He would lose much of His following. If He answered no, He could be accused of subversion. But our Lord saw through the scheme, responding neither yes nor no. Instead, He asked to have a look a the coin used to pay the tax. It carried Caesar's image and the proper inscription.

To make His point, Jesus asked of His inquirers whose image it was. They had to admit that it was Caesar's. The very fact that they had a denarius ready at hand implied that both Herodians and Pharisees were quite reconciled to living under the rule of the Emperor, as represented by his image on the coin of the realm.

Jesus, however, moved beyond this point of springing their trap. He took the occasion to set forth a principle that is very dear to all Lutherans. We speak of it as the doctrine of the two kingdoms. This is a way of referring to the fact that, as citizens of our country, we live in two sets of relationships to God. On the one hand, like all other human beings, we are God's creatures and so live under the authority of government. Luther used to call this the kingdom of God's left hand, consisting of the arrangements we call orders of creation (or preservation); namely, the state, the economic or social order, and the family (marriage). However, we are also God's children by baptism. In that respect we are different from those who have not accepted Jesus as their Savior. In this sphere we come under God's rule of the right hand: assembling to worship Him, to make use of Word and Sacrament as God's means of grace, and then move out from our gathering here to serve our fellow human beings as Christians and not just as citizens.

These two relationships are referred to in the text: "Render to Caesar the things that are Caesar's, and to God the things that are God's" (Mark 12:17 RSV). We take as our subject:

God and/or Caesar

This subject, in turn, may be considered under the three headings of duality, diversity, and duty. These items are of special significance to us as Lutherans on the day that marks the anniversary of our nation's independence.

I. Duality

God, of course, is one. Yet He works with us in two ways. On both fronts He is opposed by the same enemy who once moved some Herodians and Pharisees to put Jesus to the test.

It is Satan's business to destroy or to distort whatever God sets up for our good. He and his fellow "anarchs of the night" are at all times determined to upset civic order, which is one of God's great undeserved gifts.

Luther reminds us of this in his explanation of the petition, "Give us this day our daily bread." Here is how he puts it in his Large Catechism:

> This petition is especially directed also against our chief enemy, the devil. For all his thought and desire is to deprive us of all that we have from God, or to hinder it; and he is not satisfied to obstruct and destroy spiritual government in leading souls astray by his lies and bringing them under his power, but he also prevents and hinders the stability of all government and honorable, peaceable relations on earth. (III:80; *Triglot Concordia,* page 721)

These words from Luther provide a profound insight into the duality of our relationship to God as it involves what our text refers to with the word "Caesar." For the demonic forces that lie just beneath the surface of any civic order are anxious to upset and even destroy what God has established to keep us from having to live by the law of the jungle. That is to say, Satan is very much given to overcoming the rule of God's left hand under which we live as citizens.

At the same time, he is even more devoted to the task of leading you and me into unbelief. In that way he hopes to cut us off from the other set of relations we live with as God's children. For, once he accomplishes that, he has us in his power for good, unless, of course, God in His grace restores us to faith in Him as both our Creator and Redeemer.

It may be useful to say, in passing, that many people from other denominations call us Lutherans schizophrenic when we talk about these two sets of relationships. They say that splits up life into two compartments. But those who talk this way ought to reflect on the fact that in our everyday life we meet, let us say, a nurse who is also a mother or a policeman who is also a father. Both of these work and live in two sets of relationships: one at home, the other in their respective professions. Such duality does not make them schizophrenic. The two sets of relationships are, in most cases, improved by the very fact that they are lived out by the same person.

Our text speaks of our responsibilities to Caesar and to God for the purposes of distinguishing between them in real life. Luther used the terminology about the two kingdoms chiefly for the purpose of keeping the Gospel pure, by pointing out the difference between God's goodness and His grace.

II. Diversity

We proceed then to consider the diversity in our relationship to God as His creatures and as His children. Here we may distinguish the subject in terms of mode, content, and reach.

A. Mode

As children of God we are members of the church. One of the symbols of the church at work is the chalice. It depicts the way the church works as it proclaims not only God's Law but especially the forgiveness we have in Jesus Christ. Grace and mercy are the watchwords of God's people when seen in this relationship.

Caesar, government, operates very differently. The state deals in matters of justice, political freedom, and what the preamble to the Constitution of the United States refers to as "the general welfare." That requires legislation with the power to see things done or to leave them undone. The symbol of the government, therefore, is the sword (cf. Romans 13:4).

If men were not at heart evil, there would be no need for Caesar. But, in point of fact, men must be constrained and guided in their civic responsibilities by all kinds of laws and ordinances. Saint Augustine put it like this: "Governments exist because men are so evil."

Caesar, therefore, raises and commands military forces. The state uses police forces to preserve order when this is threatened. It extracts taxes from us. In an open society, like ours, government has the job of balancing off the selfishness of one group against another to preserve a measure of liberty. For, at heart, the state is "organized selfishness," as Emil Brunner once put it. Its mode of operation, therefore, is far different from that of the church.

B. Content

Our relationship to God as Christians includes as a primary element, the response of worship. On this point many Christians have had difficulties in the past, when they were ordered, for example, to burn a pinch of incense to honor the statue or even the person of Caesar. Our text reminds us that we are to render to Caesar what properly belongs to the jurisdiction and demands of government. Worship is not one of these items.

It is one of the monstrous evils of totalitarianism to set itself up in the place of God and to demand of its subjects that its rulers be treated as though they were divine, with a claim on the individual's total life, including that of worship.

Our fellow Lutherans in East Germany, or in the Soviet Union, have to live with this kind of monstrous perversion. If, for example, their children are confirmed on Palm Sunday or on Pentecost, these newly confirmed persons are ordered to attend a state ceremony, called "Jugendweihe," to denounce the Lord to whom they have promised to be faithful and to rededicate themselves to Marxism. At such a point many a Christian has chosen to say with the apostles of old, "We ought to obey God rather than men" (Acts 5:29 KJV). In other words, under such circumstances a Christian must choose between Caesar and God.

Such is not the case when we in the U. S. go about our normal civic duties, such as voting, paying taxes, serving on juries, etc. We acknowledge these as the responsibilities we owe Caesar and God, since governments serve as God's instruments for justice, freedom, and order. As a matter of fact, the apostle Paul does not hesitate to speak of political rule as "God's servant for your good" (Rom. 13:4 RSV).

To sum up, therefore, there is a diversity in the content of the two relationships we have referred to as the kingdom of God's right hand and that of His left. They differ also in terms of their scope, or reach.

C. Reach

Governments belong to the arrangements God has established for this life. They are tentative. They are part of the scaffolding of history. There was no need of the sword as the symbol of power before men fell into sin; and there will be no governments in heaven. Their reach is limited to this life.

Some years ago the President offered forgiveness to those who had fled the United States during the war with Vietnam. That forgiveness was and is good only for this life in the case of the men who accepted this gesture of reconciliation. On the other hand, when your pastor speaks the words of absolution in the Communion Service, he is offering a remission of sins that reaches over into eternity. He is exercising what we call the Office of the Keys, in keeping with the words of the risen Lord, "If you forgive the sins of any, their sins have been forgiven them; if you retain the sins of any, they have been retained" (John 20:23 New American Standard Bible).

III. Duty

Our text makes it very clear that the twofold relationship in which we live is not an optional matter. The words are given in the imperative: "Render to Caesar what is Caesar's and to God what is God's." This is a command.

We may not, therefore, dismiss either the church or the state as useless and unnecesary, as Marxists do. Nor dare we follow philosophers like Jacques Rousseau, who would have us believe that "nature" is the ultimate good: a condition unencumbered by the artificialities of state and church.

Both of these institutions stand in the service of God, even though they differ greatly in their mode of operation, their content, and their reach.

In the kingdom of God's right hand we are asked to live in the response of prayer, worship, and other manifestations of our awareness that here He deals with us through His means of grace. Under His left-hand rule we engage in activities that belong to responsible citizenship.

These are not matters for our option. They are enjoined upon us by our text, "Pay Caesar what is due to Caesar, and pay God what is due to God" (NEB). As we observe this Independence Day we do so with special thanks that the "lines are fallen for us in pleasant places" (cf. Ps. 16:6). We enjoy the kind of freedom that encourages us to exercise fully the prerogatives and responsibilities pertaining to Caesar and/or God.

We may well conclude our discussion of God and/or Caesar by reminding ourselves, as Lutherans, that the doctrine of the two kingdoms is a major contribution to the preservation of the kind of freedom we are accustomed to celebrate each Fourth of July. Taking this teaching seriously keeps the church from acting like a state, and government from being run like a church. A confusion of the elements in the two relationships to God in which we live as Christian citizens will in time result either in tyranny or anarchy. From these we ask God to preserve us as we observe the anniversary of our independence and continue to render to Caesar and/or God the items that pertain to each. Amen.

Martin H. Scharlemann

Related Scripture readings

Ex. 34:6-7	Ps. 90	Rom. 13:1-7	1 Tim. 2:1-6
Deut. 8:10-12	Ps. 122:6-9	Titus 2:11—3:8	

Suggested hymns

"Before the Lord, We Bow"
"God Bless Our Native Land"
"God, Lord of Sabaoth, Thou Who Ordainest"
"Grant Peace, We Pray, in Mercy, Lord"

LABOR DAY

Labor for the Lord

1 COR. 15:58

Since 1894, Labor Day has been a tradition in which people everywhere pause to honor working people. It is a holiday that is celebrated in many countries around the world.

For the Christian, it is an opportunity to thank God for the resources He provides. It is a time to remember the blessings of productivity that are ours from our Creator.

Labor Day is also a time to remember that God has placed us here to work. We are not on earth to be lazy. Luther reminds us of this in the introduction to the Ten Commandments. The First Table of the Law points us to love and service to the Lord. The Second Table of the Law directs us to love and service to our neighbors. The Christian in the world is not to be idle.

St. Paul understood very well that we who are in Christ are to abound in the work of the Lord. Perhaps the Corinthians had some of the same problems we face. Some people got the notion that Christianity was some sort of "pie-in-the-sky," other-worldly religion. Maybe some of the people at Corinth had the idea that, since they had eternal life and since the Lord could return any day, they did not need to get involved with working in this world.

In this first letter to the Corinthians the apostle Paul tries to straighten out this thinking. In chapter 15 he begins by reminding his readers that Christ has been raised from the dead. He continues by declaring that just as the Lord had victory over death, so also does God bring victory to His people through Christ. Paul says, " 'Death is swallowed up in victory.' 'O death, where is thy victory? O death where is thy sting?' The sting of death is sin, and the power of sin is the Law. But thanks be to God, who gives us the victory through our Lord Jesus Christ" (1 Cor. 15:54b-57 RSV), quoting Is. 25:8 and Hos. 13:14.

But Paul does not stop with thoughts of eternal life. He gets practical and applies Christ's victory over sin to everyday life. "Therefore, my beloved brethren, be steadfast, immovable, always abounding in the work of the Lord, knowing that in the Lord your labor is not in vain" (1 Cor. 15:58 RSV). The apostle echoes the Lord's teaching that His followers are not of the world, yet they are in the world (John 17:15-16).

As we celebrate Labor Day, it is important to look at our labor as God looks at it. Do you drive a delivery truck? Are you a housewife and mother? Are you a teller at a bank? Do you work in an office? Are you a teacher, a lawyer, or a plumber? Whatever we do, our work is labor in the Lord, when the Lord is present in our lives. Do you feel lost in the millions upon millions who make up the labor force? Do you feel that you are just an extension of a machine or an organization? Does it sometimes feel like you are just an impersonal, unimportant member of the working world? St. Paul says, "No way, my friend!" You are special. You are important. God has placed you and me here on this earth. He has given us resources of time and energy. We belong—not just to a company or a union—we belong to God. He has given us life itself. He expects us to be productive. As St. Paul reminds us, we are challenged to abound always in the work of the Lord (1 Cor. 15:58). The New English Bible puts it this way: "Work for the Lord always, work without limit."

Why is it that we tend to forget about our work as the Lord's work in the world? Why is it that we so often lose sight of the fact that we are in this world to serve God and to serve our fellowman? We tend to get caught up in other goals for our labor. We work for money, for so-called security, for the "comfortable life."

The problem is the problem of sin. St. Paul gets right to the problem. He reminds us that we have failed before God. Our sin has separated us so far from our Creator that our lives are out of touch with Him. Our labor is separated from God's purposes, because we are separated from God. The power of sin is the Law. God's law condemns us. We look at God's will for our lives, and we come away shocked at the deplorable condition of our lives. We see the materialism that has become a false god. We see how our priorities often put God at the bottom of the list. Sometimes we do not include God at all. We measure our lives according to God's expectations, and we see again and again how we have failed our fellowman. We have frequently overlooked the needs of those around us. We have often hurt those who desperately need our love, a kind word, a smile, a gesture of encouragement. We look at the Lord's desire for our lives, and we are reminded of the times when we didn't want to get involved. We are reminded of the hollow excuses we have given. We are reminded of all the opportunities of labor for the Lord—all the opportunities we have missed because, as often is the case, the opportunities came disguised as hard work. We are reminded that the flesh has so often ruled, sin has sometimes conquered, and Satan has had his way with us.

However, Paul points to God's victory: "Thanks be to God, who gives us the victory through our Lord Jesus Christ" (1 Cor. 15:57 RSV). Through His Son, God has come into this world to deal with our sinful flesh. Jesus Christ has broken the chains of sin that would keep us shackled to selfishness. Jesus Christ brings us victory, because He has fulfilled the Law. He has lived the perfect life that our Creator demands. He has restored to us the right relationship with God, who placed us here to serve Him and His creation.

Let us say that a man named John W. Fredericks robbed a supermarket and killed five people in front of a dozen witnesses. He stole a car to get away and kidnapped a child. He was captured and went to trial. The witnesses testified. He pleaded guilty as charged and received the death penalty. It was a clear, open-and-shut case. Fredericks went to prison and awaited his execution. Soon the day arrived for him to die. Then, just before his death, the governor came and gave him full pardon. He was guilty but was pronounced pardoned. He could go completely free.

This story isn't true. It just doesn't work that way. The law just doesn't let people go free in spite of their actions. They pay the penalty. That's the way it works with the law. That's the way it works with God's law.

But Jesus Christ fulfilled the Law. He took our sins upon Himself. His death was in punishment for our sins. And He was raised to life in a victory that sets us free to labor for the Lord. The resurrected and living Lord lives in the lives of His people. We don't just work day to day in a meaningless drudgery. We don't have to be depressed by what seems to be a poor-paying job. We don't have to feel there is no purpose to our jobs. We belong to Christ. His victory is ours because we are His. We are His people who live in the world for Him. There is a divine purpose in who we are and where we work. We are part of God's plan for the assembly line, the classroom, the construction crew. Whatever we do, let us engage in God-pleasing work as His special people.

In Baptism, God calls us to be His own. He makes us part of His family. The forgiveness of sins for which Christ paid on the cross becomes ours, personally. In Baptism our relationship to God is restored. We no longer are separate. As we live in the waters of our baptism, we live in the forgiveness of sins. As we live in the forgiveness of sins, we live in relationship with our Creator. We live no longer for ourselves but for Christ, who for our sake died and was raised again to victory (2 Cor. 5:15).

Jesus Christ calls us to action. Every day is a labor day for the Lord. Whatever we do, we dedicate it to the service of God and our fellowman. God places us in the community of believers, the church, to be a mighty army in this world. We are to be a powerful force for the cause of Christ. In the fellowship of His people the Lord serves the meal of forgiveness, Holy Communion. As we gather in that Word and Sacrament, we experience forgiveness of sins and strength for a life of labor dedicated to the Lord. The Lord's Supper is the Christian's labor union. It's a time of repentance. It's a time when we are united to God. We are brought back into relationship with God. We are restored into relationship with our fellowman. The stage is set for labor, for service, for action. The world would call it a union. We call it Communion.

We Christians are gathered around the Word and Sacrament, and then we are scattered into the world to be salt, light. If our job is God-pleasing it is not insignificant, no matter what we do. We are God's representatives. In His work no job is menial, useless, or low on the social scale. Even a situation of unemployment can be God's way to provide opportunity for you to represent Him and His work to those around you.

The resurrected, victorious, and living Lord calls us to labor in love. Jesus Christ commands His disciples to take up their crosses and follow Him (Matt. 10:38). The Son of God who brings us forgiveness and frees us to serve Him reminds us to work while it is day, because the night is coming when no one can work (John 9:4). Labor for the Lord is our opportunity to be God's people in the world. We share His love. We serve our fellowman.

What a privilege we have this day, to gather around the Word and Sacrament. What a great opportunity it is for us to worship the Lord who calls us to serve Him. Our lives can become a rat race of activity. It is a blessing to pause from our labor to get God's perspective. It is significant that God's Word reminds busy people like us, that He has plans for us. It's not the first time you know. Moses was busy with his flocks (Ex. 3:1); Saul was busy searching for his father's lost donkeys (1 Sam. 9:3); Elisha was busy plowing with a team of oxen (1 Kings 19:19); Nehemiah was busy working for the emperor (Neh. 1:11); Amos was busy watching his sheep (Amos 1:1); Peter and Andrew were busy with their nets (Matt. 4:18); Matthew was busy collecting taxes (Matt. 9:9); Paul was busy persecuting Christians (Acts 8:3).

It was this Paul who, stopped in the middle of a busy schedule, became a laborer for the Lord. It is this Paul who wrote our text to busy Corinthians. The same Lord who stopped Paul calls to us as we pause from our labors and celebrate Labor Day. The same Christ calls us to make every day a "labor day" for Him. "Therefore, my beloved brethren, be steadfast, immovable, always abounding in the work of the Lord, knowing that in the Lord your labor is not in vain" (1 Cor. 15:58 RSV). Amen.   Kent R. Hunter

Related Scripture readings

Prov. 16:3	Luke 14:27-35	John 17:15-16	James 2:26
Matt. 5:16	Luke 17:33	Rom. 6:5-10,22	Rev. 3:15-16
Matt. 10:38	John 9:4	Rom. 15:17	Rev. 14:13
Luke 9:18-26	John 12:23-26	2 Cor. 5:14-21	

Suggested hymns

"Take My Life and Let It Be"
"I Gave My Life for Thee"
"Let Us Ever Walk with Jesus"
"May We Thy Precepts, Lord, Fulfill"
"My God, My Father, While I Stray"
"Come, Follow Me, the Savior Spake"
"Jesus, I My Cross Have Taken"
"My God, My Father, Make Me Strong"
"Hark! the Voice of Jesus Crying"
"Soldiers of the Cross, Arise"
"Onward, Christian Soldiers"
"Before the Lord We Bow"
"To Thee, Our God, We Fly"

MEMORIAL DAY

What Memorial Day Means to Me

1 JOHN 3:16

What Memorial Day means to me I think it must also mean to you.

It may be totally a reflection of Jesus Christ and an expression of our faith in Him and of our reverence for God, our heavenly Father, to keep, or celebrate, national days like Memorial Day.

As a matter of fact, not to do so—one could argue—would be an expression of ingratitude and indifference to God and to our fellowmen, and that would not be walking by the Spirit in imitation of Jesus Christ.

What Memorial Day means to me, possibly more superficially or on the surface, is the opportunity it offers to be proud of national roots, to display some patriotism, to think for a while about citizenship and its responsibilities, and to thank God for this our native land.

We do this occasionally through the use of the Pledge of Allegiance, but most emotionally through our national hymns. So we sing with considerable feeling,

> God of our Fathers, whose almighty hand . . .
> Your love divine has led us in the past;
> In this free land by You our lot is cast.

And

> America! America! God shed His grace on thee
> And crown thy good with brotherhood
> From sea to shining sea

As a day of patriotism, Memorial Day means to me that every generation and every era is beholden to those that preceded it, and that what we do today will be influential on the generations that follow us. Memorial Day helps me to see the significance of my place in time. How I live today, in the light of the past, reflects on the future.

History stands out on Memorial Day, and I am reminded to see my place in history somewhat more clearly. I am not a biological accident of birth. Already in my mother's womb God knew me and called me by name.

What Memorial Day means to me goes back as well to its origins— origins associated with the Civil War.

At first called "Decoration Day" after the custom of decorating the graves, Memorial Day was observed for several years after the Civil War by various states, North and South, in remembrance of those who died in America's bloodiest war.

Then in 1868, May 30 was proclaimed Memorial Day by General John A. Logan of the Grand Army of the Republic. This military directive became the standard for the nation so that, today, nearly all states observe the date as Memorial Day.

So on this weekend we honor America's patriots, especially those who gave their lives for their country—from the day on which Nathan Hale faced the King's hangman with words now immortal, "I regret that I have but one life to give for my country," to the present, when devoted citizens of our nation do their duty in turn in military and civilian walks of life for the benefit of the nation as a whole.

Memorial Day means something else to me. It is a special day on which to remember loved ones and friends with whom we have walked the pilgrimage of life, who now are at rest with their Lord. For some of us the lists are longer and getting longer each year. Perhaps some of us will visit the grave of someone this weekend.

Memorial Day should bring to remembrance as well that the bells will toll someday for us—taps will be blown, as it were, when our day is done and the trumpets sounded when we shall rise in Christ. And another hymn's melody and words reverberate as with sweet joy and solid triumph we sing,

> For all the saints who from their labors rest,
> Who Thee by faith before the world confest,
> Thy name, O Jesus, be forever blest.
> Alleluia! Alleluia!

Memorial Day means all this to me—and more.

Memorial Day must also be a day for me to remember, be grateful for, and emulate the sacrificing spirit underscored this day. Way beyond the sticky sentimental, the bittersweet nostalgic, and the earthy instinctual, Memorial Day shapes genuine love. It speaks of sacrifice. And we think of the greatest sacrifice of all. "Hereby perceive we the love of God," says the apostle John, "Because He laid down his life for us" (1 John 3:16 KJV).

God takes no chance that we will misunderstand love or spoil it. In Christ He puts the principle simply. God's divine arithmetic is so elementary that even a child may understand. In fact, to understand we must become as children.

Christ took the Ten Commandments and reduced them to two: "Love the Lord thy God with all thy heart . . . love thy neighbor as thyself" (Matt. 22:37, 39 KJV). On the night of His betrayal He said: "As I have loved you . . . love one another" (John 13:34 KJV). Then He went to the cross and in deed illustrated perfectly what He commands in word.

We need that. We need both Christ's command and His example. It is not simply, "Do as I say." It is "Do as I do." Christ Himself leads us to battle and to overcome the devil, the sinful world, and our sinful flesh, even as men are led on the battlefield by their leader in front of—not behind—them.

Cynics have scorned Christ's way because people try to live their way. No age has gotten away from it, this obsession to put self first. It is the basic sin. Ancient peoples spoke their proverbs to warn of greed's danger. The Romans made the Mediterranean Sea into a Roman lake and took from their acquaintance with it a warning, "Wanting money is like drinking sea water; the more you drink, the thirstier you get." The Arabs looked to their sand dunes and put it another way: "All sunshine makes a desert." Today, wanting and having more "bread and circuses," our lives display the slogan in largest letters, "We're number one."

So we too run the risk of becoming cynical because we have seen Christ's way rejected by so many. Cynicism replaces our faith too as we replace Christ's way with our own.

But the way of Christian love is still the perfect way. Knowing God's love in Christ, you and I have the motivation to ask, not "What shall I get?", but "What shall I give?" It is in God's giving to us in Christ that we receive again.

Only one who knows Jesus Christ as One who gave His all for us, only he understands the high demands of the ringing call, "Ask not what your country can do for you, but ask what you can do for your country."

Only one who knows Jesus Christ as the One who prayed in the agony of Gethsemane, "Not My will, but Thine, be done" (Luke 22:42 KJV), only he wrings the cynicism out of "Ours not to reason why, Ours is but to do and die," and ascertains that in the valley of sarifice humanity has been lifted to new heights.

Only one who has been drawn to Christ, who said, "I, if I be lifted up from the earth, will draw all men unto Me" (John 12:32 KJV), only he recognizes the terrible centricity of "meism" and feels the fineness of pouring oneself out in service to someone else and, in the end, finds happiness.

What Memorial Day means to me, then, is more than expression of patriotism, or plumbing the meaning of supreme sacrifice, or remembering loved ones at rest with their Lord.

Memorial Day most of all is the day on which to remember that the values we hold most dear spring from one source: sacrificial love. That sacrificial love has its greatest example in God's love for us in Jesus Christ.

We need that sacrificial love, for we are at odds with God and out of synchronization with others. The golden ring of total peace on the merry-go-round of life seems to evade us, no matter how we lunge for it. Our sins are over our heads. We are restless.

God deals with our restlessness. Selflessly God puts aside His just requirements for us. We are really unable to understand that. Human economy requires debts to be paid. Like our sins, God's economy is also over our heads.

But God does not overlook our sins. He put them on His Son, and sacrifically put His Son on the cross for us. It cost God everything. That we can understand. A little piece of sacrifice by others on our behalf, if not supreme, has touched each of our lives. From our human situation we can relate to and understand that "greater love hath no man than this, that a man lay down his life for his friends" (John 15:13 KJV).

Now the feeling of being overwhelmed is complete. Overwhelmed by our sins, our hearts are restless. Overwhelmed by His love, our hearts are at rest in our Lord.

As God changes us with this perfect love, He gives us the means to change the world. Hereby we perceive that "we ought to lay down our lives for the brethren" (1 John 3:16 KJV).

So two figures loom large in my remembrance on this Memorial Day. There is the figure that possibly best shapes the goodness and greatness of America and its peoples—the Statue of Liberty, which Emma Lazarus makes to say:

> Give me your tired, your poor,
> Your huddled masses, yearning to breathe free,
> The wretched refuse of your teeming shore.
> Send these, the homeless, tempest-tossed to me,
> I lift my lamp beside the golden door.

And there is Jesus Christ, who stands with the Light of His life and His Word, showing the way—Jesus Christ, who stands at the golden door of the abundant life, here and hereafter—Jesus Christ, who says: "Behold, I stand at the door and knock; if any man hear my voice, and open the door, I will come in to him, and will sup with him, and he with me" (Rev. 3:20 KJV).

He has the right to stand there at your heart and at mine to show us the way, to ask of us that we pledge our allegiance to Him as we walk toward the sunrise of eternal life with Him. He has the right to ask of us such citizenship, because He has shown us all what it means to be His friends. He is our Great Emancipator, who has freed us forever from slavery to sin and to ourselves.

No song is more associated with Memorial Day than the "Battle Hymn of the Republic." In my mind's eye I can see the soldiers in blue singing about their Civil War campfires:

> As He died to make men holy
> Let us die to make men free.

I snap to—and come back to the present, to hear the refrain once again, but slightly changed,

> As He died to make men holy
> Let us *live* to make men free.

I look up to Christ, who died and rose for me. I look around to serve others through Him, for He died and rose for them too. We are all His friends and, through Him, friends of each other. That, ultimately, is what Memorial Day means to me. Amen.   Leland Stevens

Related Scripture readings

Prov. 14:34
Matt. 22:15-22 (Mark 12:13-17;
   Luke 20:19-26)
Mark 13:3-13 (Matt. 24:2-14;
   Luke 21:7-19)

Rom. 13:1-13
Eph. 5:1-20
Col. 3:9-17
1 Peter 2:11-25

Suggested hymns

"Before the Lord We Bow"
"God Bless Our Native Land"
"Lord, While for All Mankind We Pray"
"For All the Saints"

MOTHER'S DAY

Partners with the Lord

1 SAM. 1:26-28

In His final moments on the cross Jesus had time for few earthly concerns. Yet one of those concerns, strong enough to invade His suffering, was His love for His mother. With such a precedent we do well to pay special tribute to mothers as partners with the Lord. And not only "biological" mothers but also the fine Christian women who have never had children themselves and yet have been as important to children and other adults as natural mothers and fathers have been. For these few minutes let's think especially about mothers as partners with the Lord and thank God for all of those other partners too.

At one time it was taken for granted that everybody would probably marry and have children. It was a kind of social security system. Children assured standing in society, were workers to help support the family, and were obligated to care for their aged parents as long as they lived.

Parents as Partners

Hannah, the mother of Samuel, is an example of a woman who wanted so badly to be a parent that it seems she could think of little else. It's almost as if she were in mourning before Samuel was born. She prayed so fervently that Eli the high priest accused her of having had too much to drink.

God did answer Hannah's prayer and she didn't forget that she was a partner with the Lord. The name Samuel means "I have asked him of the Lord" (1 Sam. 1:20 RSV).

Hannah's partnership with the Lord didn't stop after the birth. As soon as Samuel was old enough, she took him to the high priest and said, "I have lent him to the Lord; as long as he lives, he is lent to the Lord" (1 Sam. 1:28 RSV).

Parents as Partners in Giving Life

There are still a lot of Hannahs around, in spite of the high abortion rate and in spite of the number of couples who choose not to have children. Many are thrilled to be able to have a child, whether by birth or through adoption.

Parents as Partners in Sharing God's Presence

Believers and unbelievers alike have the desire to marry, have children, care for them, and raise them. Only believers can catch the vision that they are partners with God and that they are actually sharing their children with the Lord. When believing parents realize that partnership, they can pass on a glimpse of the Lord to their children—a glimpse of the Lord, because, since the fall into sin, none of us knows Him as fully as our first parents did.

When Moses, Elijah, and Isaiah saw the Lord, it was only as He passed by, because they could have not stood before all of His glory. Isaiah, for example, cried out that he was a man of unclean lips as he came into the presence of God. There is a barrier between us because of our sinfulness, a barrier that Jesus Christ has removed and that will be gone fully when we stand with Him before His Father's throne.

Meanwhile, even in our imperfection we get a glimpse of the Lord from each other, and many of us had our first glimpse of Him from our mothers. Think of where you first heard of Jesus as your Savior. It may have been as your mother held you on her lap and read simple Bible stories to you or told you in her own words about how God loved you so much that He sent Jesus for you.

For little children, mothers often are the link of security and love that will later be felt for God in adulthood. Have you ever seen a little girl lost in a big department store? She may simply cry over and over, "Mommy! Mommy!" as she looks around frantically for her lost mother. When her mother comes along and sweeps her up in her arms, things are all better for her because she is found. No matter where she is, she is with her mother. She is safe.

As that mother rushes to find her, she drops everything else for the sake of her daughter. Sometimes the urge may be to say, "You naughty child, why did you wander off from me?" Probably, all of us who are parents have done something similar. But as we pass on that glimpse of God, we show our love and our concern just as He did when we strayed from Him and He reclaimed us without making us pay a price that we could not pay. He paid the price through His Son.

That doesn't make sense if you are only interested in getting something back for what you give. It does make sense to God and it makes sense to the Christian parent who is willing to give of herself for her child.

Parents as Examples of Christian Living

King Solomon was faced with a difficult choice as two women came before him and both claimed a baby as her own. Both had a child at about the same time but one child died. Now Solomon had to say which was the real mother and which one wasn't. He ordered that the living child be cut in half with a sword and shared with both mothers. One woman said, "Go ahead." The other woman said, "No, give the child to her." Solomon said that the real mother was the one willing to give the child up rather than see it killed. She was willing to sacrifice her own happiness for the sake of her child (1 Kings 3:16-28).

Have you ever felt guilty because you would really like to give up everything for your children? There is a difference between mindlessly giving up everything for children and living the new life in Christ. The two women who appeared before Solomon demonstrate opposite points. The one who says, "Kill the child," is the kind of person who doesn't want anybody to have more than she can have herself. Perhaps a little bit of her is found in each of us. God in Christ has shown us how to give of ourselves because His Son gave everything that He had. He gave His life and He gave it even though so many of us reject Him.

A Christian mother recognizes that her children are not her property. They are a trust from the Lord. Even though Hannah had wanted Samuel so badly, she knew that she had to set aside her own interests, just as the woman before Solomon did and just as so many other parents have done through the centuries.

Think back into your own life for the times that a parent sacrificed for you and did it so gladly that you didn't even know that it was a sacrifice at the time. Think too of times in your life when you have done the same for another person and not even thought anything of it because it seemed the natural thing to do.

Many of us can trace our ability to give, to love, to touch, to pray, to our mothers through the power of God's Holy Spirit. St. Paul urged young Timothy to cling fast to the faith that his grandmother and mother first had (2 Tim. 1:5). Timothy's grandmother Lois and mother Eunice will be remembered until the end ofthe world becuase they shared their faith with each other and with Timothy. Truly, they were partners with God and they are partners with mothers of all ages.

Probably, when they sat with Timothy, they weren't thinking of any time other than right then. But they were providing hope for the future. They were providing the foundation that would carry Timothy through life and into eternity. And in doing so their names would be recorded for all of us to use as examples for our lives. Not because they are so different from any of the rest of us, but because they are so similar.

Lois and Eunice helped prepare Timothy for a time when the world would seem to be tumbling down around his head. Paul himself was a prisoner and warned Timothy that he would have to suffer, but he knew that he could endure it because from a child he had known the Scriptures which lead "to salvation through faith in Christ Jesus" (2 Tim. 3:15 TEV).

Hannah, Lois, and Eunice—mothers living as partners with God—were acutally providing hope for the future even when there seemed to be no hope.

At one time Jean-Paul Sartre believed that life was absurd and without hope. He attracted many followers. They haven't spent enough time around Christian mothers who have ministered softly, quietly, gently to their children. These Christian mothers know what it is to have hope as they take a precious little gift from God who is not able even to hold his or her head up and see in that child a Christian adult who will live a life in faithfulness to God.

Mothers have looked at their infant children and seen all sorts of images: the president of a great country, a pastor, a teacher, a skilled worker, a loving mother or father, a great athlete. But there can be no greater image than that of a partner with God who helps others catch a glimpse of the Lord, who is able to share himself or herself with others, and who gives hope for the future because of Jesus Christ.

Parents as Partners in Christian Mission

Mothers who catch that vision are partners in the Christian mission. Hannah never gave up that partnership. We are told that each year she made a coat for her son and brought it to him when she and her husband came to make sacrifice (1 Sam. 2:19). Even though she didn't own her son, even though she had lent him to the Lord, she still felt her ties with him. The bond that was forged with the Lord in her prayers before Samuel was born was never broken, even though she was physically separated from her son.

Many of you can probably feel the same kind of bond with your own mothers or with children. You may do things similar to what Hannah did. How do you observe Christmas, Easter, other holidays? Like your parents did? If you think about it, you may be able to see the link that goes from your grandparents to your parents, to you, and even to your children. All of you are partners in the Christian mission. And it may be such a part of your life that you don't notice anything out of the ordinary.

As partners with the Lord you are partners into eternity. Often that may be forgotten in the routine of the day. But a mother who shares her life and love in Jesus Christ is preaching as eloquent a sermon as the mightiest spokesman for the Lord. When His disciples were going to turn the little children away from Him, He said, "Let the children come to me, and do not hinder them; for to such belongs the kingdom of heaven" (Matt. 19:14 RSV).

Our society has great admiration for an athlete who makes much money and for others who make it to the top. It may be well to admire them. But the mother who holds a child close and tells the simple story of Jesus and what it means to live in Him is doing as much in life as anybody ever can.

When we are partners with the Lord, it means that He takes our shortcomings, our sins, upon Him, and we share in His perfection. All of us probably would like to be better than we are; but Christ is the perfect One, and we can glory in this, that He has made us partners with Him.

Life in general does not give us examples of how such a partnership works—except in situations such as a mother-child relationship. Otherwise, there is profit motivation. God gave so much and receives so little in return. And yet whenever we spend time feeling guilty because we can do so little for Him instead of getting on with the task of living out our partnership with Him, we are wasting our time.

Don't expect to be perfect. In spite of the fact that she gave her son back to the Lord, Hannah was far from perfect. She was a person who lived a life surrounded by jealousy and petty bickering so similar to what occurs today. What made Hannah special was her understanding of her partnership with the Lord. That was a gift of faith.

Recognize your own shortcomings, but also marvel in what can be because of what Jesus Christ has done. Have you ever watched a mother bird tirelessly fly back and forth to her nest to feed her young? She does that because of the instinct that God gave her. To us it seems miraculous and yet dreadfully routine.

Our own lives may seem dreadfully routine too, but they are touched by the miraculous—the miraculous lived out in routine—not simply instinct, as with the mother bird, but much more, because Jesus Christ has lived for us and made it possible for us to touch each other with our lives.

Think about that today. If you are a parent, think of your own role. If not, think back to what God has made possible for you. Think of how you can share in giving life, share God's presence, and share Christ's mission. And say a prayer of thanksgiving for all the partners with the Lord. Amen.   Ronald W. Brusius

Related Scripture readings

| Prov. 14:1 | Prov. 31:10-31 | John 19:24c-27 | Phil. 4:4 |
| Prov. 23:22 | Is. 66:13 | James 1:17 | |

Suggested hymns

"Oh, Blest the House, Whate'er Befall"
"Let Us Ever Walk with Jesus"
"Lord, Thee I Love with All My Heart"
"Our Father, by Whose Name"